The Story of th

The Story of the Thirteen Colonies

by H. A. Guerber

ISBN-13: 9781511762991

Printed in the United States of America

Contents

PREFACE.

This book is intended as an historical reader, an elementary text-book in the history of our country, or as an introduction or supplement to any of the excellent text-books on the history of the United States now in use.

The aim has been not only to interest children in the great men of their own country, but to stimulate them to the cultivation of the lofty virtues of which they read, and to instil within their hearts a deep love for their native land.

All the main facts in our early history have been given as simply and vividly as possible, and the lessons of patriotism, truthfulness, courage, patience, honesty, and industry taught by the lives of our principal heroes are carefully enforced. Great pains have also been taken to relate all the well-known anecdotes and quote the famous speeches which are so frequently alluded to in our current literature.

Although this book ends with the Revolutionary War, the story of our country is continued on the same lines in a companion volume entitled "The Story of the Great Republic;" yet each book is independent of the other and can be used separately.

So simply worded as to be easily intelligible to average children of ten or twelve years of age, the text is further arranged in short paragraphs, to facilitate its use as a reader in large classes.

The pronunciation of difficult proper names is indicated in the text, and, more fully, in the carefully prepared index. The system of diacritical marks used is explained on the first page of the index.

HINTS FOR TEACHERS.

The best results in reading can often be obtained by the teacher's reading a chapter first, while the pupils closely follow the text in their own books. When called upon to re-read the same passages, it will be noticed that they almost unconsciously imitate every inflection they have heard. Thus they soon learn to read with due regard to expression, and therefore take a livelier interest in the subject-matter.

Aside from its use as a reader, this text can also serve to supply themes for daily language work, certain parts of the lesson being chosen for verbal and others for written reproduction. My experience has been that after reading the chapters over once or twice most children remember both facts and names. If they cannot do it at first, they may easily be trained to do it by the judicious stimulus of a little praise, and the hope of winning their teacher's approval.

To fix important facts in the memory, and to serve as reviews of previous readings, I have found that a set of question cards is almost invaluable. These can be quickly distributed among the children, who are called upon to answer them verbally or in writing, as best serves the teacher's purpose at the time.

Pupils consider historical matches even more exciting than spelling matches. To vary recitations, matches can be conducted in various ways. For instance, all the question cards bearing upon the parts of the book already perused can be divided between the two "sides." The pupils furnish oral or written answers, the side answering most questions correctly reaping the honors. The match can also be carried on by the teacher's supplying names or dates, and requiring pupils on alternate sides to state clearly what they know in connection with them. At other times, ordinary quiz methods can be used, or the teacher can relate some fact or anecdote, calling upon different pupils to supply the purposely omitted names or dates.

Children are also often deeply interested in verbal pictures. For example, the teacher, without mentioning name, time, or place, can describe Franklin flying his kite, Ethan Allen surprising the garrison at Ticonderoga, Columbus at La Rabida, etc. The description ended, each pupil can write down the names of the characters described, and mention time, place, and any other fact the teacher calls for. Such historical riddles seem more like play than work to the average child, and before long all take great pride in making verbal pictures of their own, to be guessed by their schoolmates, or handed to the teacher instead of an ordinary composition. Such work not only appeals to childish imagination, but cultivates memory and attention while firmly fixing important facts in youthful minds.

To encourage a taste for poetry and rouse a love for the beautiful by fine descriptions of the noted characters or great events with which the pupils have just become familiar, it is often well to read aloud some of our most famous songs or poems.

It is universally conceded that history and geography should go hand in hand; so suitable maps have been supplied, upon which children should be encouraged to locate each spot as soon as it is mentioned. The teacher should also procure a blank map for each pupil (such as the Eclectic Map Blanks, American Book Company), so that, after finding any place named on the ordinary map, the pupil can locate it exactly on an outline map. Many children are greatly interested in marking the names themselves as soon as their attention is drawn to them, and take great pride in seeing their maps grow. This method is often more helpful than any other in making children see how civilization has spread and what changes have gradually taken place in our country.

To fix upon their minds the fact that colonies were planted by different European nations, it is often advisable to purchase at a stationer's tiny adhesive stars of various colors. Each color serves to represent a nation, and stars are pasted upon the spots where colonies once stood. In cases where colonies proved unsuccessful, a black star can be pasted over the colored one, but in such a way that enough of the original star remains to show to which nation the colony once belonged. Where colonies changed hands several times, stars of appropriate colors can be pasted overlapping one another. This work fascinates children, and as the stars are adhesive, it can be done in class with very little trouble. A little tact on the teacher's part will make each pupil strive to have the neatest and most accurate map.

History and geography, when studied in their turn, will seem far more attractive to children if these methods have been pursued; for many persons and places already familiar will then be joyfully greeted as old friends.

THE THIRTEEN COLONIES BEFORE THE REVOLUTION

STORY OF THE THIRTEEN COLONIES.

I. OUR COUNTRY LONG AGO.

Learned men, who read the story of the earth in the mountains, valleys, rivers, lakes, and seas which cover its surface, tell us that America, although known as the New World, is really older than Europe. The sun has shone upon this continent and the rain has watered it for more centuries than we can count. If you study your maps carefully, you will notice lofty mountains, great lakes, and long rivers in many parts of the country; and you will see that it is beautiful and fertile almost everywhere, except in the far north, where snow covers the ground most of the year.

The same wise men who found out that the country is so old, dug down into the soil, examined the things they found there, questioned the Indians, and, little by little, discovered that our continent has been inhabited by many different kinds of animals and men. They found huge bones of animals which died thousands of years ago, and placed these in museums, where you can now see them. They also found the bones of some of the ancient men and women, with some of their weapons, tools, kitchen pots, and bits of their garments.

By studying these things very carefully, and by listening to the stories of the natives, they learned a great deal about the country which, from Greenland and A-las´ka in the north, to Cape Horn in the south, was once inhabited by tribes of Indians. None of these had white skins like the inhabitants of Europe, black skins like the negroes in Africa, or yellow skins like the Chinamen in Asia. But as they were more like the people in Asia than like those in Africa or Europe, some men now think they may once have belonged to the same family.

A Savage Indian.

Still, the men living on our continent were so unlike others that they are called red men, and form a race by themselves. Those who lived in the part of the country which is now called the United States had copper-colored skins, high cheek bones, straight, coarse black hair, small black eyes, and very wide mouths. Although they all looked somewhat alike, they were very different in their ways of living. The Indians living east of the Rocky Mountains were a little more civilized than those living west of those mountains and in the far northern parts of the continent.

A Wigwam.

The western and northern Indians are generally called savage Indians, for they lived by hunting and fishing, had no houses like ours, and were always roaming around in search of game. They were sheltered from the sun and rain by tents called wigwams. These rude dwellings were made by driving poles in the ground, in a circle as big as the wigwam was to be. When all the poles had been set up, the tops were drawn close together and firmly tied. Over these slanting poles the Indians spread the skins of the animals they had killed, or else they wove leaves and branches between the poles to form a thick screen. The space between two of the poles was left open to serve as a door, and over this was hung a bear or buffalo skin to keep out the sun, rain, or cold.

The space inside the wigwam was generally very small; but all the family crowded in, and when it was cold or wet, a fire was lighted in the middle of the floor. The smoke then escaped through a hole purposely left in the top of the wigwam, or through the open door.

The savage Indians had learned to make baskets, which they plastered with clay inside and out, and dried in the sun until they could hold water. When they wanted to boil their meat or to warm water, the women, called squaws, heated stones in the fire, and then dropped them into the water, which was thus brought to a boil.

These Indians rowed about in canoes made of basket work, of birch bark, or even of hollow tree trunks. As they had only stone axes, they could not easily cut down trees, so they brought them to the ground by kindling a fire all around them. When the tree had fallen they built another fire farther up the trunk. A log of the right length having thus been secured, they hollowed it out by starting small fires on top of the trunk, and scraping away the charred wood, until the log formed a rude canoe.

The Indians made their birch-bark canoes by sewing long strips of bark together with plant fibers or the sinews of the animals they had killed. The basket-work canoes were covered with skins to make them water-tight.

Making a Canoe.

II. THE BARBAROUS INDIANS.

The Indians east of the Rocky Mountains knew a little more than the savage Indians, so they are called the barbarous Indians. Besides hunting and fishing, they dug up roots with stone hoes, or with shells, and planted corn, beans, pumpkins, squashes, tomatoes, tobacco, and sunflowers. Of course they did not have neat fields and gardens, such as you see now; but they scratched a hole wherever the ground seemed good enough, dropped a few seeds into it, and covering them over, left them to grow without further care.

Indian Pottery.

The barbarous Indians were not content, like the savage Indians in the West, to fling a skin around them to keep off the cold, merely fastening it with a big thorn to hold it together. So they made winter garments by sewing skins together with sinews or plant fibers. In summer they had lighter clothes, rudely woven out of cotton or plant fibers. They, too, wove baskets, made beautiful birch-bark canoes, and after fashioning pots and pans out of clay, hardened them in the fire, so that they could use them in cooking.

These Indians had tools and weapons made of finely polished stone or bone, and they liked to live in villages. Instead of wigwams, many of them built houses of wood, or basket work and clay, roofed over with strips of bark. Sometimes the roof was a very thick layer of long grass, laid on rude rafters, and held down by poles to form a kind of thatch.

A Long House.

The houses thus built were generally very long and rather narrow, with a door at either end, and a passageway running through the center. On either side of this hall there were little rooms, each occupied by a family. At intervals along the passage the ground was hollowed out, and a clay or earthen fireplace was built, where four families cooked their meals. Above the fireplace there was a hole in the roof to serve as chimney. The rooms near the doors were generally used as storerooms for food and fuel. When several of these long houses were built together, they were often surrounded by a wooden wall, or palisade, to keep out the wild beasts and to serve as protection in time of war.

The Indians who once lived in New York and in the valley of the St. Law′rence lived in long houses, but the Mis-sou′ri Indians had round houses, built of the same materials. In the round houses the fireplace was in the middle, and families lived in rooms shaped like cuts of a pie. Many of these round houses were built close together, and then surrounded by a palisade made of tree trunks. These were driven into the ground so close together that they formed a very strong fence.

Although Indians did not have family names, such as we have now, each great family, or clan, had a special sign whereby it was known, such as a bear, a turtle, or a beaver. This sign was often marked upon their bodies in bright colors, and they carved and scratched it on all their belongings. From this sign the family was known as the bear, the turtle, or the beaver clan. Each clan selected a ruler, called sachem, or sagamore, whose orders all obeyed, and they also chose a chief to lead them in time of war.

The Indians had never been told about the God we love, so they worshiped the sun, moon, and stars, the lightning and thunder, the wind and rain, and said that one great spirit, called Man′i-to, was always watching over them. They also believed that when they died they would be carried off to a place where they could hunt and fish forever, and they called this heaven the happy hunting grounds.

Their religious ceremonies were usually performed by Indians called medicine men. These pretended to be very wise, and frightened the others by dancing and yelling wildly, and using strange words and signs. They said this would please their gods, and drive away the evil spirits of sickness, storm, or drought. The Indians were so simple that they believed all this nonsense, and they were so afraid of evil spirits that they often begged an animal's pardon for killing it. You see, they thought the spirit of a wolf or bear might else be so angry as to torment them in their dreams!

A Papoose.
The men spent their time hunting, fishing, and fighting, but left all the rest of the work to the women. When they moved from one place to another, the squaws had to carry all the household goods, as well as the papooses, or babies. But the men carried only their bows and arrows, hunting knives, and the hatchets called tomahawks, which they threw with great force and skill.

III. THE MOUNDS.

Besides the savage Indians of the north and west, and the barbarous Indians of the east, there were also half-civilized Indians in the south of our country. They dwelt not only in what is now New Mex′i-co and Ar-i-zo′na, but were also found in Mexico, Central America, and South America, as far down the map as Chile (che′lā).

The southern Indians had learned how to build canals, so as to lead the water far away from the streams into dry and barren lands. When the ground had thus been watered, or irrigated, it became very fruitful, and they could grow all the grain and vegetables they needed.

The southern Indians lived together in huge fortresses, built of sun-dried bricks, called adobe. These fortresses were large houses five or six stories high, containing ever so many little rooms, each occupied by one family. Thus one house often sheltered two or three thousand people.

Cliff Dwellings.

Sometimes these Indians built their houses on the ledges of steep rocks, or canyons. Such houses were called cliff dwellings, and many remains of these queer homes are still found in the southwestern part of our country. The Indians who lived there were gentle, and not fond of fighting, but they built fortresses and cliff dwellings to defend themselves when attacked by the savage Indians.

You see, the savage Indians did not grow any grain or vegetables, but they came down from the north to steal the provisions of the southern Indians. These, therefore, carried all their supplies into the cliff houses, which they built in such a way that it was almost impossible for an enemy to get in them.

The inhabitants themselves, however, easily went in and out by means of ladders, which led from story to story, or from ledge to ledge. Their houses had no doors down near the floor, but were entered by a hole in the roof.

In each of these fortresses there was a great cistern, full of water, and so large a supply of food that the Indians could stand a long siege. In times of danger they pulled all their ladders away up out of reach, and when their enemies tried to climb the steep cliffs or straight walls, they pelted them with stones and arrows, and thus drove them away.

Wise men tell us that even before our country was occupied by the savage, barbarous, and half-civilized Indians, whose way of living has just been described, it had been inhabited by their ancestors or by an older race of men. We know they existed, because people have dug up their bones. These have been found principally inside huge earthen mounds of very queer shapes. The mounds were evidently built by those early inhabitants, who are hence known as the mound builders. Trees hundreds of years old now grow upon these mounds, which are found in most parts of the eastern Mis-sis-sip´pi valley, especially in O-hi´o.

In one place you can see a big mound representing a snake one thousand feet long, his body lying in graceful curves along the ground. This snake's mouth is wide open, and he looks as if trying to swallow an egg-shaped mound, which is one hundred and sixty-four feet long, and hence a pretty big mouthful. As this mound is so odd, it has been inclosed in a park, where it is to be kept just as it is, to remind people of the mound builders who lived here so long ago.

No one now knows exactly why these queer mounds were made, but learned men have dug into about two thousand of them, and as they have generally found bones, stone arrowheads and axes, beads, mortars, hammers, tools for spinning and weaving, pottery, baskets, and coarse cloth, they think the mounds must have been intended principally as burying places. The beads found in them are very like those which the barbarous Indians called wampum and used as money. Indians wore these beads in strings around their necks, or wove them into belts, using beads of different colors to form very pretty patterns.

Wampum.

IV. WHERE THE NORTHMEN WENT.

As you have seen in the first chapters of this book, America was once a very different country from what it is to-day. Now you are going to learn how it changed, little by little, from the wild land where Indians roamed about in the huge forests covering the greater part of the country, into a civilized country.

We are told that in all the wide territory now occupied by the United States, there were, four hundred and fifty years ago, about two hundred thousand Indians. These were very few inhabitants for so big a country, for now there are many cities here which count many more citizens.

The Indians then little suspected that on the other side of the great ocean there was another country, occupied by a race of white men, who knew much more than they did, and who were soon coming to take possession of their land.

But the people in Europe, wise as they were, did not know many things which everybody knows now. That was not their fault, however, for they had been trying for several centuries to learn all they could. In the middle of the fifteenth century Europe was already an old country, where long series of kings and queens had ruled over the people. There were then in Europe cities more than two thousand years old, ancient temples and castles, and many of the beautiful Christian churches which people still admire, because none finer have ever been built.

The people in Europe had long been great travelers by land and sea, although it was not so easy to get about then as it is now. Indeed, on land they could go only in wagons, in litters, on horseback, or on foot; and on the water they used nothing but rowboats or sailboats, because no one had yet imagined that one could use steam or electricity. On the sea, even the boldest sailors did not dare venture far out of sight of land, for fear they would not be able to find their way back.

The best seamen in Europe were the Northmen, or vik´ings. Already in the eighth century they used to sail out of the *viks*, or bays, in Nor´way, every spring, to go in search of adventures. These Northmen, Norsemen, or Normans, little by little explored the coast of the North Sea, and of the Atlantic Ocean, and finally came to the Strait of Gi-bral´tar. Passing through this opening, they came to the beautiful Med-i-ter-ra´ne-an Sea, where they cruised about, even visiting the Greek islands and the renowned city of Con-stan-ti-no´ple.

As you will see by looking at your maps, this was a very long journey for men who had nothing but sailboats or rowboats, such as very few sailors would dare to use nowadays. But the Northmen were afraid of nothing, and when the wind blew, and the great waves tossed their little vessels up and down like cockleshells, they held tight to the rudder and steered on, singing one of their famous songs.

Sometimes, however, the tempest raged so fiercely that they were driven far out of their course. Thus, in the middle of the ninth century, one of these hardy seamen, after tossing about on the stormy seas several days, landed on an island which he had never seen before.

A Viking.

This new place was Ice´land, and he was so pleased
with his discovery that he sailed home and persuaded his family and friends to go back

11

there with him to settle down. In a few years other Northmen came to live in Iceland, sailing across the Atlantic from time to time to visit their old homes and friends. Soon the colony grew so large that its seamen kept up a lively trade with different ports in Europe.

One of these Ice-lan´dic seamen, Gunn´biorn, on his way home, was once overtaken by a violent storm. It drove him far out of his course, and finally brought him in sight of a new land, covered with snow, which he called the White Land. When he reached home he told the Ice´land-ers what he had seen; but no one cared then to go and see if there really was a land west of Iceland, as he had said.

About a hundred years later another man, Er´ic the Red, was driven out of Iceland for murder. Remembering what Gunnbiorn had said, he sailed westward, and went to settle in the new country, which he called Greenland, so as to attract other settlers. A number of them soon joined him there, and began to trade with the Es´ki-mos, a race of Indians who lived in the coldest part of the country, where they hunted white bears and fished for cod and seals.

V. THE NORTHMEN IN AMERICA.

After Eric the Red had settled in Greenland, he sent word to one of his friends, Biar´ni, to come and visit him. Biarni gladly accepted the invitation, and although he had none of the instruments which sailors now use to guide them safely over the seas, he set out boldly, steering his course by the stars.

Unfortunately for Biarni, a storm soon came up. The stars could no longer be seen, and his ship was driven far out of its way. When the skies cleared Biarni saw land before him, and fancied he had reached Greenland. So he sailed slowly along the coast, looking for Eric's settlement; but, as he could not find it, he soon turned around and went back to Iceland.

Of course he told his adventures to his friends, and Leīf the Lucky, hearing him describe the land he had seen, set out in search of it, in a large ship manned by a number of men. Sailing westward, Leif coasted along Lab-ra-dor´ and No´va Sco´tia, came to Cape Cod (map, page 189), and landed, it is thought, somewhere in Rhode Island, in the year 1001.

Although Biarni and Leif did not know it, they had been the first white men to see North America, which, as you will see, did not receive this name till many years later. Leif the Lucky found so many wild grapes in this region that he called the country Vine´land, and loading his ship with timber and grapes, he went home. But he, with another Northman, soon came back to spend a winter in the new country, where the climate was much milder than in Iceland or Greenland.

For some years ships sailed from Norway to Iceland, from Iceland to Greenland, and from Greenland to North America, where a Northman finally settled with about one hundred and forty men and women. Snor´ri, the son of this brave leader, was the first European child born in America. He lived to grow up, and the great sculptor Thor´wald-sen, as well as several other noted men, claimed him as one of their ancestors.

The Northmen, however, had a very hard time in America, for they were soon attacked by the Indians, whom they called Skrae´lings. Even the women had to fight to defend themselves against the savages. But when they found that these attacks did not cease, they decided to leave the country, and went home in 1012.

A Viking's Ship.

As far as we know, after that no ships from the North visited America for several hundred years. But the story of Eric the Red and of Leif the Lucky was, fortunately, written down in one of the old Norse tales, or sagas. It is probable that the people went on talking for some time of the strange country their friends had visited, but after a while they forgot it entirely. Indeed, were it not for the old story, no one would now know that they were the first Europeans who set foot in our country, and you will still hear some people deny that they ever came here.

Now, it may seem very strange to you that the news of the Norse discovery of the new land was not made known everywhere; but you must remember that the people in Europe had no newspapers or printing presses, and that news traveled very slowly. No one but a few Northmen, therefore, were aware that land had been found in the West.

So America was forgotten until, according to an old story, a Welsh prince named Mad'oc was driven across the Atlantic by a storm, in the twelfth century. He was so well pleased with the new country he found that he is said to have left some of his men there, promising to return soon with more settlers. The story goes on to say that he sailed from Wales to keep this promise, but no one ever heard anything more of him, or of the men he left in America.

Some people think that he and his men perished in a storm, and that the settlers he left behind him were murdered by the Indians. Others insist that the whole story was made up by the Welsh, so they could claim the honor of having discovered America. Whether the Welsh ever came here or not,—and it is hardly likely they ever did,—the fact remains that our continent, after being discovered by Europeans, was lost again.

VI. QUEER IDEAS.

People living in Europe, near the sea, were all fond of cruising about; but as they had no compass at first, they seldom ventured out of sight of land, for fear of losing their way. After a time they learned to steer their vessels by means of the stars; but as these could serve as guides only on clear nights, sailors were glad to use the compass when it became known in Europe, in the twelfth century.

But although seamen now fearlessly cruised about the European waters, they did not venture far out into the Atlantic, which was then known as the "Sea of Darkness." The fact is, they were afraid to do so, because they had been told they would meet strange monsters there, such as mermen and mermaids. They also thought their vessels would be drawn toward the "Loadstone Mountain," a great magnetic rock which would draw all the nails out of their planks, and thus make their boats fall to pieces.

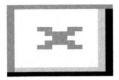

Of course this was all nonsense, but most of the seamen believed these tales as firmly as some sailors now believe that Friday is an unlucky day; and as no one had ever gone far out in the Atlantic, even learned men could not prove to them that they were mistaken. Besides, although they had fairly good maps of the countries they had visited, people knew nothing at all of the rest of the world. Their maps showed only the northern part of Africa, the western and southern parts of Europe, and the western part of Asia. All the rest was a blank.

Common people then believed that the earth was round and flat, like a pie, with the ocean flowing all around it. So they were afraid to venture too far out, lest they should fall over the edge of the world and drop down into space! Wise men, however, already knew better; for, about three hundred years before Christ, Greek philosophers had begun to suspect that the earth is round like a ball, and not flat, as every one until then had supposed.

They and their pupils wrote books giving their reasons for believing this; but as printing was not invented till seventeen hundred years later, these works were known only to a few learned men. Most of the European scholars then lived in Greece or Constantinople, and kept these precious manuscripts in monasteries or private libraries, or in palaces and schools.

In the twelfth century a Spanish-A-ra'bi-an philosopher read some of these Greek manuscripts, and then wrote a book, saying that he not only believed that the earth is round, but that he thought it would be possible to sail around it! This statement, so natural and simple now, seemed so absurd to the people who heard it then that they began to make all manner of fun of it. They asked how it would be possible for a ship to sail uphill, even supposing it did not tumble off the earth when it reached the edge, which they called the jumping-off place.

They also asked how the trees on the other side of the earth could grow with their roots up in the air, and inquired whether the rain and snow flew up instead of falling down. These questions, which seem so odd now, were very natural, for people did not then know, what your teachers have explained to you, that the earth is like a big magnet. It holds fast everything on its surface, and nothing can fall off, even though it spins around and around, and whirls through space much faster than the fastest express train can travel.

The Turks, who were not Christians, besieged the city of Constantinople in 1453, and when they became masters of it, and of the surrounding country, the learned men all fled, taking with them many of their precious manuscripts. Deprived of their quiet homes, and in many cases forced to teach to earn their living, these wise men settled in various cities, where they imparted to others all they knew.

As printing had just been invented, books, instead of being worth a fortune, soon became so much cheaper that almost everybody could afford to have one or two volumes. The precious manuscripts the wise men had saved from the Turks were therefore printed, and people soon began to talk about the strange things they read in them, and longed to know more.

VII. PRINCE HENRY THE NAVIGATOR.

Among the first books printed were the accounts of the travels of two daring men, Mar´co Po´lo and Sir John Man´de-ville. These men had visited many of the countries of the East, and the first had even gone to China, which was then called Ca-thay´. The stories these travelers told were so interesting and exciting that people became anxious to visit these strange countries, and especially to trade there and thus grow rich.

Ever since the days of Al-ex-an´der the Great, if not sooner, a certain amount of trading had been done with the East. But as all the silk, sugar, spices, etc., had to be brought by coasting vessels to the head of the Per´sian Gulf or the Red Sea, and thence overland by caravans to some port on the Black Sea or the Mediterranean, they became very costly.

A Caravan.

Sometimes, too, the goods were brought all the way from China or India, or the heart of Africa, through deserts and over mountains to the Black, the Mediterranean, or the Red Sea, by caravan, although it took a long while to travel all those weary miles.

For some time the Turks allowed this trade to go on, but by and by they began to treat the traders so badly that the traffic almost stopped. The cities of Ven´ice and Gen´o-a in Italy, whose ships had constantly sailed to and fro in the Mediterranean and Black seas, to carry these goods from port to port, were now nearly idle, and the people who had grown so rich were about to become poor.

As the Turks were too strong to be driven away, the traders longed to find another road to reach India, Cathay, and Ci-pan´go, or Japan. A way of reaching these countries by sea was what they most desired, because it is much easier to carry goods in ships than on camels.

The Ve-ne´tians and Gen-o-ese´, however, were not the only ones who wished to find a new road to the East. Many of the European coast cities fancied that if they could only discover it, they could keep the trade all to themselves, and thus grow richer and more powerful than their neighbors.

One of the countries which most coveted the Eastern trade was Por´tu-gal, where a bright boy was heir to the throne. This lad, Prince Henry of Portugal, once went with his father to Ceu´ta in Africa. Although then very young, he listened eagerly to the wonderful stories told about Guin´ea, on the southern side of the Sa-ha´ra. He soon began to wonder if it would not be possible to get there by sailing along the coast instead of crossing the African desert. This, you must know, was a great undertaking, because people found nothing to eat or drink there, and suffered much from the heat. Besides, the wind called the simoom raised such clouds of dust that whole caravans were sometimes buried in the sand.

By looking at the maps in your geography, you can see that it was easy to sail from Portugal to Guinea; but at that time people knew nothing of the west coast of Africa. Prince Henry, in hopes of solving the problem, began to study very hard. Before long he read in an old book that a wise man thought it possible to sail all around Africa, and he longed to find out if this was true.

As soon as he grew up, he therefore hired a number of seamen to try it, and showed such interest in sea voyages that he is often called the Navigator. The mariners thus sent out, little by little explored the coast of Africa, and creeping farther south every journey, they discovered the Ma-dei´ra and Canary Islands.

But the sight of the smoke above the volcano of Ten-er-ïfe´ so terrified them that they dared go no farther. It was only some time later that Por´tu-guese mariners reached the Cape Verde Islands and Sen-e-gal´. But one of their number had in the meantime learned, from a Flem´ish seaman, that there was a group of islands westward, and the Portuguese, going there, planted a colony on the A-zores´, which still belong to them.

VIII. YOUTH OF COLUMBUS.

While Henry the Navigator was busy with his discoveries, the rest of the world was not standing still. Although he little suspected it, a boy born in Genoa, about 1436, was to be a far greater navigator than he. This boy was Christopher Columbus.

Although Christopher's father was only a poor wool comber, he managed to send his son to school at Pavia (pah-ve´a). There the little fellow studied hard. But he had no pretty books such as you have now, and had to pore over musty parchments. In spite of that, he took special interest in geography and mathematics. When only thirteen, Christopher was forced to leave school, because his father could not afford to keep him there any longer. After combing wool for a short time, he went to sea with one of his relatives.

A sailor at fourteen, Columbus began to lead a very stirring and adventurous life. Genoa, his native city, was then often at war with other places, and battles were fought on the sea as well as on land. Besides, in going about from place to place, Genoese vessels were frequently overtaken by pirates; so mariners in those days had to know how to fight, as well as how to sail their vessels. Columbus, therefore, had more than one battle with these sea robbers, whose aim was to secure the goods on board his ship. Once he took part in a fight off Cape St. Vin´cent. Here, his vessel having caught fire, he and his crew sprang into the sea to escape the flames. By rare good fortune, Columbus managed to grasp a floating oar, and with this slight help he swam to the distant shore.

In the course of his many journeys Columbus visited all the principal ports of the Mediterranean Sea. Ever eager to learn, he questioned the seamen and travelers he met, and they gladly told him the strange things they had seen and heard while visiting foreign lands.

After a time Columbus came to Lis´bon, hoping to be employed in making discoveries for the crown; for, as we have seen, the Portuguese were the boldest seamen of the day. Whether or not Columbus took part in some of their journeys we do not now know; but we do know that he soon found himself obliged to earn his scanty living by drawing maps. As he was a very pious man, he daily went to say his prayers in a neighboring convent church, where he met a young lady whom the nuns were educating. Falling in love with her, Columbus soon made her his wife.

The newly married couple lived with the mother of the bride, the widow of a seaman and chart maker. She soon gave her son-in-law her husband's papers and instruments. In looking over the former, Columbus found that his wife's father had once been in the employ of Henry the Navigator, and had written an account of his voyages.

Poring over these papers, and thinking over all he had read and heard from travelers, Columbus became more and more convinced that the earth is round, and that by sailing directly westward one would reach the coast of Asia. This idea, which had already haunted him for some time, now left him no rest He longed to try, for he was in hopes of finding a new road to India, which would enable his native city to carry on the trade which had made it so rich. This trade had been stopped, when he was about seventeen, by the taking of Constantinople, as you have already heard.

According to the calculations of Columbus,—for, like all the wise men of his time, he fancied the earth smaller than it is,—the lands known to the Europeans extended over about two thirds of the surface of the globe. As he thought that Asia stretched much farther east, he now began to think that perhaps the strip of ocean which separated Cipango from the Canary Islands might not be so very broad, after all.

To discover whether others shared this belief, Columbus wrote to Tos-ca-nel'li, a learned Italian, asking him whether he thought it possible to reach Asia by sailing straight across the Atlantic. Toscanelli answered that he thought it could be done. He also sent Columbus a map he had drawn, on which he had placed Cipango (Japan) nearly on the spot which Cu'ba occupies in your geographies.

When Columbus received this map he determined to make an attempt to reach Asia by boldly sailing westward. But he was too poor to buy or hire a vessel himself, and we are told that when he once asked the Genoese to supply him with one, offering to give them the benefit of his discoveries, they only made fun of his plans.

Although disappointed, Columbus did not give up his idea, and still tried to gain all the information he could. He even made a journey to Iceland; but the people he talked with there had so entirely forgotten the land that Eric and Biarni had visited in the west, that they never even mentioned it to him, so far as we now know.

IX. COLUMBUS AND THE QUEEN.

Genoa having refused to help him, Columbus, some time later, explained his wishes to John II., the new king of Portugal, for Henry the Navigator was dead. This ruler also took great interest in such matters, but as he was not very wise himself, he called together a council of his most learned men to listen to all that Columbus had to say. These men declared the plan absurd; but the king did not feel quite sure that they were right.

John did not wish any other country to have the glory of finding the new road to India; still, he did not want to trust a ship to Columbus. Advised by one of his bishops, he secretly sent out a light ship, with orders to sail directly westward. The captain and crew did not believe one could sail across the Atlantic, and were sorely afraid of the monsters which they fancied swarmed in the Sea of Darkness. They therefore took advantage of the very first storm to come back, reporting that it was impossible to go any farther.

When Columbus heard that the king had been so dishonest as to try to steal his ideas, he was justly indignant. He left Lisbon in anger, vowing he would have nothing more to do with such a ruler. Still, as he was fully determined not to give up his cherished plan to try himself, he sent his brother Bar-thol'o-mew to England to ask if Henry VII. would give him a ship.

In the meanwhile Columbus staid in Spain, earning a scanty living for himself and his little son Diego (de-ā´go); for by this time his wife had died, leaving him alone with this child. But although so poor that he often had to beg food, Columbus thought night and day of the time when he would sail westward to Asia. As he went from place to place, he tried to interest various people in his plans, and for a while believed that some Spanish noblemen would help him.

V. Brozik, Artist.

Columbus at the Court of Ferdinand and Isabella.

But they finally told him they could not undertake such an important expedition, and advised him to apply for aid to the king and queen at Cor´do-va. Hoping still, Columbus journeyed thither, and found that the royal couple were too busy trying to drive the Moors out of Spain to pay much attention to him.

Time went on thus, and while Columbus was anxiously waiting, Portuguese seamen crept down the coast of Africa until they reached its southern point. There a tempest raged so fiercely that the captain called it the Cape of Storms, and, not daring to venture around it, sailed home. When he told John II. of his discovery, the king declared that the cape should henceforth be called the Cape of Good Hope, for there were now good prospects of reaching India by coasting all around Africa.

In 1487, the very year that the Portuguese thus finished exploring the western coast of Africa, Columbus was called before the learned men of the Spanish court at Sal-a-man´ca, to explain what it was he wanted to do.

But after talking about his plan for three years, these men also declared it was impossible, because one of the fathers of the church had said that the earth could not be round. Columbus was in despair, for he had spent years in trying to convince them, and in following the court from one city to another.

Greatly discouraged, yet determined not to give up, Columbus decided to leave Spain and go to France to seek help of the French king. He therefore set out on foot for the nearest seaport, but on the way thither stopped at the monastery of La Rábida (rah´be-dah) to ask for a drink of water and a bit of bread for his hungry boy.

While the child was eagerly eating the food given him, the prior, or chief of the monastery, passed by. Struck by the noble appearance of Columbus, he began to question him. Columbus then told Prior Perez (pā´reth) how much he longed to carry out the plan upon which he had set his heart.

La Rábida.

The prior, who was a learned man, listened with great interest to the tale Columbus told. He also invited the travelers to tarry with him a few days, and sending for his friends, bade them hear what the stranger had to say. Among the listeners were the brothers Pinzon (peen-thōn´), experienced seamen from the neighboring port of Palos (pah´lōs).

The prior and the Pinzons were so impressed by all Columbus said that the latter offered to furnish a ship and go with him, provided he could secure enough help to carry out his plan. As for the prior, he offered to go to court and persuade Queen Is-a-bel´la—whose confessor he had once been—to supply the necessary funds.

True to his resolve, the prior rode off on his mule, and laid the whole subject so simply and plainly before Isabella that she promised to give all the help needful. This answer so pleased Perez that he wrote to Columbus, "I came, I saw, God conquered," and sent him money, bidding him come to court without further delay.

It seemed at first as if Columbus's troubles were now over; but in spite of all Isabella's good will, some time passed by before she and King Fer′di-nand could hear him. Then, more delays having occurred, Columbus set out, in disgust, to try his luck elsewhere. But Isabella, fearing that the chance of great wealth and honor would escape her, sent a messenger after him, saying she would even pledge her own jewels to raise the necessary sum. Hearing this, Columbus came back, and only with great difficulty secured a royal promise that he should have the title of admiral, that he and his descendants should govern any lands he discovered for Spain, and that he and they should receive one tenth of all the pearls, gold, and spices brought to Spain from these new countries.

X. "LAND! LAND!"

In 1492, therefore, more than eighteen years after he began asking for help to carry out his daring plan, Columbus sailed out of the port of Palos with three little vessels—the *Santa Maria* (sahn′tah mah-ree′ah), the *Pinta* (peen′tah), and the *Niña* (neen′yah). Columbus himself commanded the first, the Pinzon brothers were captains of the other ships, and the crews, all told, consisted of about one hundred men.

The vessels were small and uncomfortable, without real decks, cabins, or holds; but Columbus started out boldly to brave unknown dangers and venture into strange seas. His course was first southward, because he intended to get fresh water at the Canary Islands before sailing due west in search of Asia.

The Santa Maria.

Although still in well-known waters, the seamen already seemed doubtful and afraid, and the third day after they sailed, the *Pinta* signaled that there was something wrong. Columbus soon learned that her rudder was out of order; and although Pinzon tried to mend it, his vessel could not sail fast.

When Columbus came to the Canary Islands the rudder was properly repaired, and while waiting for that to be done, he heard from the inhabitants that after strong westerly winds they had often found on the beach strangely carved bits of wood. Once two bodies were washed ashore, and the islanders said they were those of men unlike any race ever seen in Europe or the parts of Asia and Africa with which they were familiar.

Setting out from the Canaries, Columbus quieted the fears of his crew, when they came within sight of Mount Tenerife, by explaining to them that it was only a volcano, like Mount Et′na. Then he steered directly westward.

The men's hearts sank as they lost sight of land, and all began to think over the terrible stories they had heard. People who are always looking out for something to get scared at are easily frightened; so when the three ships sailed into the warm waters of the middle Atlantic, where seaweed grows in such quantity as to make the sea look green, the sailors were terrified.

But Columbus was no faint-heart, and he steered right on, making the ships cut their way through the floating masses of seaweed in the Sar-gas′so Sea, as that part of the Atlantic is called. Perceiving that his men grew more frightened as the distance increased between them and their homes, Columbus did not tell them how many miles they had

19

really gone, but carefully kept the account for his own use. To cheer his men, he promised a great reward to the first who caught sight of land.

Instead of looking for mermaids, monsters, and boiling seas, the sailors now began to watch for land, and several times they mistook clouds for distant mountain peaks. Day after day passed on, until the men, horror-struck at the endless stretch of sea and sky, again and again begged Columbus to turn around; but he always refused.

Then they grew so angry that they plotted to throw him overboard and take command of the vessels themselves. They were on the point of doing this, when they saw a shrub covered with fresh berries floating over the waters. A little farther on they found a carved stick and a small board, and soon after beheld birds flying southward. By these signs they felt sure land must be near, and eagerly resumed their watch for it.

To please one of the Pinzon brothers, Columbus unwillingly consented to change his course and follow the birds; but if he had gone straight on he would have landed in what is now called Flor´i-da.

Standing on top of the poor little cabin of his vessel, on the evening of October 11, Columbus peered out into the darkness, wondering whether he would see land before him when the sun rose. Suddenly he fancied he saw a light. He called two men, and as they saw it too, he felt sure they were near land at last.

A few hours later, at early dawn on Friday morning, October 12, 1492, the *Pinta*, which was ahead, gave the joyful signal that land was in sight. When the sun rose, all on board beheld one of the Ba-ha´mas, which Columbus mistook for an island off the coast of Asia.

John Vanderlyn, Artist.

Landing of Columbus.

Although uncultivated, the island was inhabited, and the Spaniards soon saw naked savages run out of their low huts, to stare in wonder at the ships. The poor creatures, who had never seen sailing vessels before, fancied that the boats had come straight down from the sky.

Dressed in scarlet, wearing beautiful armor, and carrying a flag which bore the crowns and initials of Ferdinand and Isabella, Columbus went ashore in a small boat. As he set foot upon land, he fell on his knees, and after thanking God for bringing him there in safety, he took possession of the island in the name of the king and queen, and called it San Salvador (sahn sahl-vah-dōr´).

His men, who had been disobedient, hateful, and ready to kill him such a short time before, now crowded around him, kissing his hands and feet, and begging his pardon for their past ill conduct. The natives, who had fled into the woods at the approach of the strangers, watched all these proceedings from behind the trees. After a short time they timidly came forward, and, encouraged by the Spaniards' kind glances, wonderingly touched the white men's hands and beards, and evidently admired their gay apparel.

Columbus was so sure he was near India that he called the savages Indians, a name which has ever since been used for the red men in America. Then he gave them colored caps, glass beads, and little bells, trinkets which the Indians fancied were priceless heavenly treasures!

XI. COLUMBUS AND THE SAVAGES.

Although Columbus could not understand one word of the language the savages spoke, and although they did not know Spanish, he tried to talk to them. As you can readily imagine, this was not an easy thing to do; but by making signs, Columbus soon made the Indians understand that he would give them more of his trinkets in exchange for fruit, a kind of bread they showed him, and the yellow ornaments they wore.

When Columbus found out that these ornaments were of pure gold, he felt more convinced than ever that he was near Cipango, Cathay, and India, and he asked the natives where they had found the precious metal. As they kept pointing southward, and said words which he fancied sounded like Cathay and Cipango, he imagined they were trying to tell him about those countries, and about a king in the south, who was so rich that all his dishes were of gold.

The desire to reach this country and to visit Asia's ruler—for whom he had brought letters from Ferdinand and Isabella—made Columbus set out early on the morrow. He took with him seven happy natives, whom he intended to use as interpreters; but they fancied he was carrying them off to heaven.

Coming to some more small islands, Columbus took possession of them also; and on the way to a larger one he overtook a savage in a light canoe. The Spaniards drew the man on board with his skiff, and as they found in the latter a gourd of water, some bread, red paint such as the savages used to beautify themselves, and a string of the beads they had brought, they concluded he was going to announce their coming to some friends.

When they drew near the coast, therefore, they sent this man ashore in his little canoe, and, landing themselves the next morning, found the savages assembled and ready to exchange gold and food for worthless European trinkets.

After visiting several of these islands, Columbus steered southward in search of a larger island, which was Cuba, but which he at first mistook for Japan. Here the savages fled at his approach; but Columbus, anxious to make friends with them, went into their huts, and left a few beads in each, forbidding his men to carry anything away.

Still searching for the wonderful city of the fabulous ruler who ate and drank from vessels of pure gold, Columbus coasted along Cuba. As he saw nothing but mean huts, he fancied that the city must be far inland, and that none but poor fishermen lived on the shore. He therefore sent an expedition inland; but his men were sorely disappointed to find a collection of mud huts instead of the grand palaces they had expected to behold.

The savages here did something which greatly puzzled the Spaniards. Taking a certain kind of dried leaf, they rolled it up, and, lighting one end, stuck the other between their lips. Then they drew into their mouths and blew out a strangely perfumed smoke! Seeing that the savages seemed to enjoy it, the Spaniards tried it also, and thus became acquainted with the tobacco plant and learned to smoke.

It was now so late in the season that Columbus did not dare to wait any longer to secure the cargo of silks, pearls, spices, and gold which he had hoped to carry home. He therefore determined to sail back to Spain, make known his discovery to the king and queen, and fit out a larger expedition for trading.

On his way home he discovered and took possession of Hāi′ti, which he called His-pan-io′la, or "Little Spain." His best ship, the *Santa Maria*, having been wrecked, forty men were left behind in a fort there. Columbus bade them be good to the savages, and learn their language, so they could tell him all about the great king when he came back.

21

XII. HOME AGAIN.

Columbus set out on his return journey in January, but he was obliged to go very slowly, because the wind was often against him, and because one of his vessels was badly crippled. In the middle of February a terrible storm separated the two ships, and Columbus, fearing his vessel would sink, and the news of his discovery perish with him, wrote out two accounts of his journey. These were inclosed in cakes of wax, which were put into empty casks. One of them was cast into the sea, but the other was left on deck, so it could float off if the boat sank.

The storm grew so fierce that Columbus and his men vowed to go in procession to the first church they saw after landing, and return thanks, if they were only spared. When the storm-tossed navigators finally reached the Azores, therefore, they tried to keep this promise; but the people were so unkind that they imprisoned those who landed. Columbus managed to recover his men, but on the way from those islands to Spain another tempest overtook him, and it was only after much tossing that the *Niña* at last reached Portugal.

The Niña.

As soon as he landed, Columbus sent a messenger to Ferdinand and Isabella to announce his safe return, and the success of his undertaking. The very people who had once made fun of him now eagerly listened to all he had to say, and their hearts were full of envy at the thought that the newly discovered islands would belong to Spain, and not to Portugal. It is even said that some one basely proposed to murder Columbus and send out ships to take possession of the land in the name of Portugal.

The king, however, would not consent, and Columbus, sailing away again, finally entered the port of Palos, whence he had started so many months before. As soon as the people heard that he had succeeded, they were almost wild with joy, and rang all the bells in the city. One of the Pinzons, who had hoped that Columbus's vessel had gone down in the storm, came into Palos just then with the *Pinta*. He had intended to claim all the honors of the new discovery, and was greatly disappointed when he found that Columbus had reached port before him.

The Pinta.

As the court was at Bar-ce-lo´na, Columbus immediately went there, with his Indians, parrots, and other curiosities, and all along the road people came in crowds to stare at him. They gazed in wonder at the Indians, who, in their turn, were bewildered by all the strange sights they beheld.

The royal couple received Columbus in state, and, after he had bent the knee before them in homage, made him sit down in their presence—a great honor—and relate his adventures. Columbus gave them glowing descriptions of the new islands, told them he had found the road to India, and promised that they should soon be rich. This news caused such rejoicing that the royal couple went to give solemn thanks in the chapel.

Honors were now showered upon Columbus, who was welcomed and feasted everywhere. In fact, people made such a fuss over him that some of the courtiers became jealous. A story is told about one of these men who sneeringly remarked at a banquet that even if Columbus had not discovered the road across the ocean, there were plenty of brave Spaniards who could have done so. Columbus seemed to pay no special attention to this taunt, but quietly taking an egg from a dish placed in front of him, he asked the guests if they could make it stand on end. All tried, and failed. When they finally declared the feat impossible, Columbus struck the egg on the table hard enough to break its shell slightly. Then, leaving it standing there, he calmly said that everything was equally easy—after you knew how to do it.

The news brought by Columbus made a sensation everywhere; but while all the people were talking about his discoveries, he was actively preparing to cross the Atlantic again, intending this time to reach India. Instead of three miserable little ships, and very small crews, he now had a fleet of seventeen vessels, carrying about fifteen hundred men.

The second expedition set sail in September, 1493, and, after stopping at the Canary Islands, steered across the Atlantic to the eastern West Indies. There Columbus found a fierce race of Căr´ibs, of whose attacks the Indians had complained to him the year before. The Spaniards explored these islands, lost their way at times in the forest, and once came to the homes of some cannibal Caribs. When they saw a heap of human bones, left over from a horrible feast, they shuddered with dread at the thought of falling into the hands of these cruel men.

XIII. COLUMBUS ILLTREATED.

About one year after leaving the colony at Haiti, Columbus came back, to find the place deserted. One of the Indians who had gone to Spain with him knew enough Spanish by this time to act as interpreter. Through him, Columbus learned that some of the colonists had fallen ill and died. The rest, disobeying his orders, had been cruel and unkind to the natives, and so anxious to get rich that the Indians, in self-defense, had fallen upon and killed them.

The site of the first colony having proved so unlucky, Columbus established the next on another spot, and called it Isabella, in honor of the queen. Here the Spaniards began to trade with the natives for gold, and Columbus sent this metal to Spain, asking that provisions should be sent out in exchange, because the Spaniards did not like the natives' food, and had not yet found time to grow crops for their own use.

Besides the gold, Columbus sent back a whole cargo of men, women, and children, to be sold as slaves. This was cruel and wicked; but Columbus believed, as most men did then, that it was far better for the Indians to be slaves among Christians than free among heathens.

The colonists had expected to grow rich very fast, and to find all the gold they wanted. They were therefore sorely disappointed at getting so little, and before long became discontented and hard to manage. While they were trading with the natives, Columbus sailed away, still seeking for India, which he felt sure must be quite near there.

He went along the coast of Cuba, and then southward to Ja-māi´ca, finding several other small islands. But after cruising about for some time, he came back to Isabella, where he found the colonists ill and unhappy. They had not only quarreled among themselves, but had illtreated the natives, robbing them of their wives and daughters, as well as taking their food.

The Indians, who had once been so happy and indolent, were now weary and sad. Besides, they had learned to hate the Spaniards, and were plotting to murder them. Learning this, Columbus had to treat them as foes, to protect the Spaniards. The natives next refused to sell any more food to their enemies, and if a provision ship had not come from Spain, Columbus and his colony would surely have died of hunger. As there was very little gold to send back this time, Columbus shipped all his prisoners of war, and thus five hundred natives were forwarded to the Spanish slave market.

During the next two years Columbus had much trouble with the Indians, who, finding it almost impossible to collect the amount of gold he exacted as tribute, often revolted. He also had a hard time managing the colonists. Homesick and discouraged, they accused him of deceiving them by false tales of the riches they could get, and of ruling so badly that their lives were in danger.

These complaints were sent to Spain, and the royal couple, hearing so much against Columbus, sent a nobleman to Haiti to find out if their viceroy was really acting unjustly. Some people say that this nobleman did not even try to find out the truth, and Columbus found it necessary to go back to Spain with him and explain matters to the king and queen, leaving Bartholomew Columbus in charge of the colony.

The second arrival of Columbus at court was very different from the first. Instead of greeting him with cheers and festivities, people now looked coldly upon him and avoided him as much as they could. It was only three years since he had discovered a road across the Atlantic; but as he had not yet brought back huge cargoes of spices and silks from India, people openly despised him.

Although this reception cut Columbus to the heart, it made him all the more anxious to reach India, the goal of all his hopes. He therefore prepared a third expedition; but this time he had so much trouble in getting funds and ships that it was not till May, 1498, that he could again set sail, with a fleet of six vessels.

Instead of taking his usual course, Columbus steered directly westward from the Cape Verde Islands, and reached Trin-i-dad' in the middle of the summer. After visiting that island, he explored the gulf behind it, and came to the mouth of the O-ri-no'co River. From the great volume of water, he concluded that this river must flow through an extensive continent, and thought it must surely be one of the four great streams from the Garden of Eden!

Although Columbus now felt certain he had finally reached the mainland of Asia, he could find none of the rich cities he sought, and sadly went back to Haiti. There things had been going on worse than ever, for the Spaniards had mutinied, as well as the natives.

Columbus now forwarded the most disobedient of the colonists to Spain. But when they got there, they complained so much about him that the king and queen again sent out a nobleman to see what was amiss. The Spanish officer no sooner reached Haiti than he took the command away from Columbus, who was put in irons and sent back to Spain to be tried there.

XIV. DEATH OF COLUMBUS.

Eight years after his first journey across the Atlantic Columbus returned to Spain a prisoner! The captain of the vessel wanted to remove his chains, but Columbus proudly said that as they had been put on by the orders of his sovereigns, he would wear them until the king and queen set him free. He also added that he would keep those chains as long as he lived, and have them buried with him, so that people might know how unjustly he had been treated. It is said that the fetters hung six years over his bed, and that, at his request, they were placed in his coffin and buried with him.

When Columbus reached Spain the sensation was great. The people, who had been at first enthusiastic and then indifferent about him, were now indignant that he should be treated so unjustly, and when Isabella received a letter, telling her how he had been insulted, her heart was filled with pity.

She immediately sent a messenger to remove Columbus's chains, and summoned him to court, where she wept with him when she heard him describe his sufferings. But although Isabella promised that his honors should all be given back to him, and that she would soon fit out a new expedition for him, she kept him waiting two long years.

In 1502 Columbus set out on his fourth and last journey, not as ruler of the new lands, but merely as explorer. After a stormy passage, he reached the colony at Haiti, where the governor refused to allow him to land. Columbus told this man that a tempest was coming up, and that it would not be safe for any one to leave the port. But the governor would not believe him, and ordered some Spanish vessels, which were laden with gold and ready to start, to set out for Spain.

They no sooner got out of the harbor than the storm overtook and sorely damaged them. But Columbus, who had warned them of the danger, safely weathered the storm, and, sailing on, he explored the coast of Central America, still seeking a road to India.

Columbus was now old and ill; so after coming to a part of the coast which he took for the Spice Islands because he found spices there, and after suffering shipwreck, he returned to Haiti and thence to Spain. There he soon heard that Isabella, Queen of Castile (kahs-teel´) and Le´on (parts of Spain), was dead, and his sorrow at her loss made his health worse than ever. The Spaniards, knowing his principal friend was gone, now treated him even more scornfully than before, and mockingly called him "Lord of Mosquito Land," because there were so many mosquitoes along the South American coast.

These insults, added to his disappointment at not finding India, helped to make Columbus's illness fatal; and feeling that he was about to die, he wrote his will, leaving his title of admiral to his son. He passed away in the month of May, 1506, saying: "Into thy hands, O Lord, I commend my spirit."

Buried at Valladolid (vahl-yah-dō-leed´), his body was removed first to Se-ville´, then to San´to Do-min´go, in Haiti, then to Ha-van´a, in Cuba, and finally, after the relinquishment of Cuba by Spain in 1898, back to Seville again. After his death, people began to realize what a great man Columbus was, and King Ferdinand, who had been so unkind to him while he lived, put up a monument in his honor, on which was later inscribed the motto: "To Castile and Leon Columbus gave a new world."

Since then, many monuments have been erected and many pictures painted of the man who, in spite of poverty, illness, and countless obstacles, never gave up his aim, and manfully strove to reach it as long as he lived. His faith, his courage, and his perseverance have served as shining examples for more than four hundred years, and although he died poor and neglected, he is rightly considered one of the world's greatest men.

XV. HOW AMERICA GOT ITS NAME.

The news of Columbus's first successful journey no sooner became known in Europe than each country wanted to secure some share of the profitable trade which they fancied would soon be opened with India. Henry VII., King of England, who had refused to listen to Columbus's plan, now hired a Venetian captain named John Cab´ot, and sent out an expedition in 1497.

Cabot crossed the Atlantic, and explored what he thought was China, but what was really part of North America,—probably the coast of New´foŭnd-land and of the mainland from Labrador to Cape Cod. Sailing along, he found a beautiful country, saw a bear plunge into the water to catch fish, and, landing at least once, planted an English flag upon our soil, thus taking formal possession of it in the name of England.

The next year his son made a similar journey. Sailing in and out of every bay, he sought a strait which would take him past these wild lands to the rich cities of the East, which he fancied were very near there. Of course he failed to find such a strait between Nova Scotia and Cape Hat´ter-as, but the English later claimed all this part of the country, because it had been discovered by the Cabots. Still, for many years they made no attempt to plant a colony there, and prized their discovery so little that Henry VII. gave Cabot only £10 reward for all he had done.

The Portuguese, as we have seen, were very jealous when Columbus came back from his first journey, saying he had found the road to India. But while he was away on his third expedition, one of their captains, Vasco da Gama (vahs´co dah gah´mah), sailing all around Africa and across the Indian Ocean, reached Cal´i-cut in India. He came home in 1499, with a rich cargo of silks and spices; and the Portuguese rejoiced greatly that they were the first to reach India by sea.

The next year some Portuguese ships, on their way around Africa, happened to go so far west that they sighted the coast of South America. Spain and Portugal had by this time drawn a line of demarcation on the map, agreeing that all lands west of it should belong to Spain, and all east to Portugal. As the new land was east of this line, the King of Portugal sent a fleet to explore it, and thus found it was a great continent. All the lands already discovered by the Spanish and English were supposed to form part of Asia; but this land was so far south that it was called the New World.

The pilot of the Portuguese fleet was a young Italian named A-mer´i-cus Ves-pu´cius. He took note of all he saw, and wrote an interesting account of his voyage. This narrative described the country, and as every one wanted to hear about the new discovery, it was soon published. A German geographer, reading the account of Americus, was so delighted with it that he suggested that the new continent should be named America, in honor of the man who had explored and described it so well. The name was thus given at first only to part of South America; but when, years afterwards, it was found that all the western lands belonged to the same continent, the whole of the New World was called America. Thus, by an accident, our country bears the name of Americus, instead of that of Columbus, its real discoverer, for it was the latter who showed the way to it, although he believed till his death that he had found only a new road to Asia.

Many writers claim that the first voyage of Americus to the West was in 1497, four years before his exploration of South America, and that he then landed on the American continent, shortly before Cabot, and more than a year before Columbus reached the mainland. According to them, Americus was thus the first to reach the continent which bears his name.

XVI. THE FOUNTAIN OF YOUTH.

The Spaniards, as we have seen, immediately began planting colonies in the West Indies, and in a few years they took possession of all the islands, and made the natives their slaves. These poor creatures were forced to work hard for their new masters, who, thirsting for gold, made them wash the sands of all their streams, and toil without ceasing.

The Spaniards in Cuba and Haiti, hearing many tales of the gold to be found in the west, soon sent out several expeditions. They also planted a few colonies along the coast of Central America, but at first these did not thrive.

Among the colonists in Haiti there was a Spaniard named Bal-bo´a. He was poor but very daring, and wished to join an expedition bound for the mainland. As he could not pay for his passage, he hid in a cask and had himself carried on board ship as freight.

When far out at sea Balboa crept out of his hiding place, won the captain's forgiveness, and soon made so many friends that he became a leader in the settlement they founded on the Isthmus of Da´ri-en, or Pan-a-ma´. After a time he learned from the natives that a great ocean lay on the other side of the ridge of mountains. He therefore made his way through the tangled underbrush and rank tropical growth, bidding his men wait at the foot of the mountain, while he climbed up alone.

Balboa Discovers the South Sea.

On reaching the top, he gazed southward and beheld a great stretch of water, which he called the Great South Sea (1513). Falling down upon his knees, he gave thanks to God, and then made joyful signs to his followers to come up and join him.

Accompanied by these men, Balboa next went down the opposite slope, and, reaching the shore, waded out into the ocean, with a flag in one hand and his drawn sword in the other. Standing thus in the waters of the Great South Sea, he took possession of it in the name of Spain, declaring that all the countries it bathed belonged to his sovereigns.

That same year one of the former companions of Columbus, Ponce de Leon, started out from Puerto Rico (pwĕr´tō re´co). Like many other men of his time, he believed that all the stories he had heard were true, and that somewhere in the world there was a magic spring called the Fountain of Youth. He thought that if one drank of its waters, or bathed in them, one would be sure to become young again, and as he was rapidly growing old he longed to find and try it.

After vainly seeking the fountain on the newly discovered islands, he fancied, from what the natives told him, that it might be situated on the mainland, so he set out in quest of it. On Easter Sunday (*Pascua florida*), he landed in a beautiful country, which, in honor of the day, he called Florida. After taking possession of it for Spain, he began exploring; but although he drank from every spring, and bathed in every stream, he could not find the Fountain of Youth, and kept growing older and older.

After several years he made another journey to Florida, to continue his search, and to make a settlement; but as there were no roads through the dense forests and treacherous marshes, he and his men suffered greatly from hunger and heat. Finally Ponce de Leon was sorely wounded in a fight with the Indians, and his men carried him back to Cuba. There he died, a wrinkled old man, still regretting that he had not been able to find the Fountain of Youth. His friends, who admired his bravery, and often said he was as bold as his namesake the lion, wrote upon his tomb: "In this sepulcher rest the bones of a man who was Leon by name and still more by nature."

While Ponce de Leon was seeking the magic fountain, some of his countrymen were exploring the Gulf coast, from Florida to Mexico, under the leadership of Pineda (pe-nā′da). In 1519, also, a Portuguese, named Ma-gel′lan, took a Spanish fleet down the coast of South America. After a time he came to the strait bearing his name, and, sailing through it, beheld the Great South Sea.

Magellan was such a brave seaman that he steered boldly across this unknown expanse of water. It was so much smoother than the Atlantic that he called it the Pacific, or "Peaceful" Ocean, a name which it has borne ever since, and which suits it much better than the one given by Balboa. After a journey of a year and a half, Magellan finally reached the Phil′ip-pīne Islands, where he was killed in a fight with the natives.

One of his officers now took command, and went on till he reached India. Thence, by way of the Cape of Good Hope, he came to Spain, sailing for the first time all around the globe. Besides proving that the earth is round, this voyage showed that South America is separated from India by a great stretch of water. Magellan's journey took three years, but now, thanks to steamboats and railroads, it can be made in about two months.

XVII. "THE FATHER OF WATERS."

The year 1519 was eventful for the Spanish. In that year Magellan started out on his journey around the world, Pineda explored the Gulf coast, and Cor′tez,—a very brave Spaniard,—landing at Vera Cruz (vā′rah croos), marched into the country and took Mexico, the city of a great Indian chief named Mon-te-zu′ma.

Although Cortez had only five hundred men, and the Indians were very numerous, he soon became master of the whole country, which belonged to Spain for many a year. The Indians in Mexico were partly civilized, and the region was rich in gold and precious stones. Another Spaniard, named Pi-zar′ro, shortly after conquered Pe-ru′, and owing to the cargoes of gold constantly sent from Mexico, Peru, and other parts of the newly discovered lands, Spain soon became the wealthiest country in Europe.

Although the Spaniards were anxious to grow rich, they also wished to convert the natives. Besides soldiers and colonists, therefore, every vessel brought out priests to convert the heathen. These men were very good, and so fearless that they went everywhere, preaching and teaching with great zeal.

They tried to learn the natives' language, and often questioned the people about the country. All that they heard they repeated to their leaders, who, finding there was much gold in the northwest, resolved to go in search of it. A party headed by Narvaez (nar-vah′eth) set out, therefore, to explore and conquer the northern coast of the Gulf of Mexico.

But Narvaez was very unfortunate. While he was inland his ships sailed on, and when he came back to the shore they were out of sight. Painfully making his way along through the tangled woods for many miles, he finally reached the coast again and built a second fleet. This, however, was wrecked at the mouth of the Mississippi ("The Father of Waters"), where Narvaez was drowned.

Four of the followers of Narvaez, narrowly escaping death, soon after fell into the hands of the Indians. By pretending to be magicians, these men made the Indians fear them. They lived eight years among various savage tribes, wandering all across the continent to the Gulf of Cal-i-for´ni-a, and finally came back to Mexico, where their leader, Cabeza de Vaca (cah-bā´sah dā vah´cah), told their adventures to the Spaniards. He was the first European to visit the region between the Mississippi and California, and it is said that he tramped more than ten thousand miles during those eight years of captivity.

The tales told by Vaca and his companions made the Spaniards long to visit the country and find the Seven Cities of Cibola (see´bo-lah), where they fancied they could secure much gold. A priest named Mar´cōs therefore set out to question and convert the natives. Taking one of Vaca's companions, a negro servant, as guide, Marcos wandered on foot into New Mexico, where he saw from afar seven Zuñi (zoo´nyee) pueblos, or villages.

Hearing from the Indians that these were the Seven Cities of Cibola, he went back to report what he had seen. A Spaniard named Coronado (co-ro-nah´tho) now set out with an army of about two hundred and fifty men. He made his way into the new country, visited the Cibola pueblos, and hearing wonderful tales of Acoma (ah´co-ma), a city built in the skies, set out to find it. After many hardships, he and his little army came into a wide valley, in the center of which rose a huge rock, with straight sides more than three hundred feet high, and with a broad flat top of about seventy acres.

On the top of this rock the Indians had built one of their cliff dwellings, which they reached by narrow rocky stairways. Coronado visited this strange city, but finding the people poor, and hearing there was gold farther north, he pressed on, and even came to the Grand Canyon of the Col-o-ra´do.

While Coronado was thus exploring much of the southwestern part of our country, another Spaniard, De So´to,—who had helped conquer Peru,—set out from Cuba with nine vessels and an army of nearly a thousand men. He landed in Tam´pa Bay, and, searching for gold, wandered for three years through the forests of Florida, Geor´gi-a, Al-a-ba´ma, and Mississippi. Often attacked by hostile Indians, and suffering greatly from hunger and sickness, he nevertheless reached the Mississippi River, and crossed it near Lower Chick´a-saw Bluffs.

But he could not find the El Do-ra´do, or "Land of Gold," he was seeking, and after exploring the region between the Missouri and the Red rivers, and losing many men, he resolved to turn back. Before long, however, De Soto died of malaria (1541), and the Spaniards, after secretly burying him, told the Indians he had gone on a long journey. But when they saw that the savages did not believe them, and gazed suspiciously at the upturned soil, they began to fear the Indians would treat De Soto's remains shamefully.

De Soto's First View of the Mississippi.

In the middle of the night, therefore, they took their dead leader up out of his grave, and wrapped him in a cloak weighted with sand. Then, rowing out into the Mississippi, they noiselessly lowered his body into the middle of the great stream which he had been the first European to visit since the Spaniards were shipwrecked at its mouth in 1519.

His little army, after making a desperate attempt to retrace its way overland, came back to the Mississippi. Here the Spaniards built huge rafts, and, floating down the stream, reached its mouth at the end of nineteen days. Then, coasting along the Gulf, they made their way to a Mexican settlement, where they told the story of all their adventures during this long search for gold.

French vs. Spanish

XVIII. THE FRENCH IN CANADA.

Columbus had been dead for nearly fifty years, and yet people were only just beginning to explore that part of the New World which is occupied by our country. But the coast of South America was quite well known by this time, and already clearly outlined on maps, while North America was still a mystery.

Most people still fancied that North America was only a narrow strip of land, like Central America. They also thought that somewhere north of the Gulf of Mexico there must be a strait, by means of which it would be easy to pass into the Pacific Ocean, and thereby reach India without taking the long journey all around South America.

The navigators who visited the coast of North America in search of this strait, spoke, on their return, of the great quantities of fish they had seen. Even the Cabots had found many fish there. Now, all the Christian people in western Europe were Roman Catholics in those days, and so ate fish instead of meat on fast days, which were so many that they took up about one third of the time. Fish was therefore in great demand.

As the rivers did not supply enough, fishing soon became a paying trade for those who lived by the sea; and because many fish were found on the coasts of Brit'ta-ny, in France, the Bret'on fishermen did a good business. Still, when they heard of great schools of codfish on the Banks of Newfoundland, which could be caught and salted very easily, these bold fishermen were anxious to secure them. They therefore began to make fishing trips across the Atlantic, and before long gave their name to Cape Breton.

France and Spain often waged costly wars, and seeing that the Spaniards received much gold from the New World, the French longed to have some of it, too. Their king, therefore, said that he had as good a right to any undiscovered land as the Spaniards, and that the latter should not be allowed to keep the New World all to themselves.

Spanish

Next, he sent out an expedition under Verrazano (ver-rah-tsah'no), who explored the coast of North America from what is now North Car-o-li'na to Newfoundland. Some historians say that this captain finally fell into the hands of cannibal Indians, who devoured him in the sight of his helpless crew; but others declare that Verrazano was caught by the Spaniards during a war with France, and hanged as a pirate.

The French were not discouraged, however. A few years after the death of Verrazano they sent out another expedition, in charge of Cartier (car-tyā´). After sailing nearly all the way around Newfoundland, this explorer, in 1534, came to the mainland, set up a huge wooden cross, and took possession of the country, in the name of France. The next year he came back, and, sailing up the St. Lawrence River, gave it that name because it was Saint Lawrence's day in the calendar. He visited the place where Que-bec' now stands, and went on up the stream until he came to an Indian village, composed of several long houses surrounded by a palisade.

Niagara Falls.

Near this village there was a hill which Cartier climbed, and when his eyes rested upon the beautiful view at his feet, he exclaimed that this was truly a Mont-re-al', or royal mountain. A city built some time after on this very spot still bears the name he gave the place.

After spending a short time on the St. Lawrence, Cartier went back to France, taking several Indians with him. Some of these savages died, and when Cartier returned without them, and tried to establish a colony, he had trouble with their relatives. Cartier gave the name of Can´a-da to part of the country, and in talking with the Indians learned that far inland there was a huge waterfall, whose roar could be heard many miles away. Indeed, some of the Indians called it Ni-ag´a-ra, which in English means "The Thunder of Waters."

Although Cartier longed to see this wonder, he had no time to visit it, and as the climate proved too cold for his men, he went back to France, saying it would not be possible to plant a colony so far north. For the next few years, therefore, the French had only a few trading posts along the St. Lawrence River, where the Indians came at certain times to exchange the furs of the animals they had killed for the beads and trinkets they loved so well.

XIX. FRENCH AND SPANISH QUARRELS.

Twenty years passed by before the French again attempted to plant a colony in America—twenty very eventful years for France and for all western Europe. The people, who, as you have heard, had all been Roman Catholics for centuries, now began to divide. Some of them refused to obey the pope, and wanted to worship in a somewhat different way. In France these people were called Hu´gue-nots, and among them was a nobleman named Coligny (co-leen´ye).

Seeing that the Huguenots were much disliked in their own country, Coligny proposed that they should go to the New World and found a colony where they could worship as they pleased without offending any one. As Cartier said the climate was too cold in Canada, Coligny sent the Huguenots farther south, in charge of Laudonnière (lo-do-ne-ār´) and Ribault (re-bo´).

The French colonists, landing in the New World, called the country Carolina, in honor of their king, Charles, and they also gave this name to their fort. But they soon lacked food and became discouraged. As the vessel in which they had come had sailed away, they built a new ship and set out for France. At sea, lack of provisions soon brought them to such desperate straits that they drew lots and ate one of their number. In fact, had they not been taken prisoners by an English ship, it is very likely they would all have died of hunger.

Two years later another French settlement of the same name was made in Florida, on the St. Johns River. As soon as the colonists were comfortably settled, Ribault went off to punish some Spaniards for attacking his fleet in time of peace. But while he was away the Spaniards came by land to surprise the Huguenot settlement.

Now, you must know that the Spaniards were ardent Roman Catholics, and believed that all Huguenots were very wicked people. Besides, they hated the French, with whom they had often been at war, and claimed Florida as their own land because Ponce de Leon had visited it first. They were so sure, therefore, that they were doing right by killing the French Huguenots, that when the massacre was all over, their leader, Menendez (mā-nen´deth) put up a sign on a tree near by, saying that he had slain the colonists, not because they were Frenchmen, but because they were not good Catholics. This done, Menendez went back to the colony of St. Au´gus-tine, which he had founded two years before (1565) in Florida. This is the oldest city on the mainland of the United States, and it still proudly bears the name given by Menendez, its Spanish founder.

Old Spanish Mission at St. Augustine.

The news of the massacre of the Huguenot colonists was received with great indignation in France. As the king would take no steps to avenge it, a nobleman named De Gourgues (goorg) fitted out an expedition at his own expense, and attacked the Spaniards on the St. Johns. He came upon them unawares, and killed them all, as they had murdered the Huguenots at the same place. Then he placed a sign above the heads of the men he had hanged, saying they had been executed, not because they were Spaniards, but because they were pirates and murderers. De Gourgues then sailed away, for the Spaniards had so strong a fort at St. Augustine that the French had given up all hope of settling in Florida.

Four years after founding St. Augustine, the Spaniards planted the colony of San Diego in California, which, however, was soon abandoned. Their next colony was started many years later at Santa Fé (fã´), in New Mexico, and thence many priests went out to build mission stations in the West and convert the Indians.

The present city of Santa Fé, the oldest town in the western United States, was founded in 1598 by a Spaniard named Oñate (ōn-yah´tā), who had married the granddaughter of Cortez, conqueror of Mexico. This Oñate had helped the Spaniards conquer Peru. He was a very brave man, and hearing about the "Sky City" of Acoma, he resolved to visit it. About fifty years after Coronado, therefore, he came within sight of the strange town perched upon a rock.

The Indians, who by this time had learned to fear and hate the Spaniards, thought this would be a good chance to kill their greatest foe. So they invited Oñate up into their city, and showed him their cisterns and granaries. Then, taking him to the top of one of their great houses, they bade him step down through an open trapdoor into a dark chamber.

Oñate, suspecting treachery, refused to enter, and it was well for him that he did so, for a number of armed Indians were lurking there in the darkness, ready to kill the Spaniards as soon as they set foot in the apartment.

XX. THE SKY CITY.

Although Oñate cleverly escaped being murdered by the Indians in Acoma, another Spanish captain, Zaldivar (thahl-de´var), was less fortunate, a short time after. He and half his force imprudently ventured up on the rock; but instead of staying together, as Oñate's troops had done, they scattered to view the strange place. The Indians took advantage of this to pounce upon their unsuspecting guests, at a given signal, and began killing them.

The Spaniards, clad in armor, defended themselves heroically; but many fell, and the last five were driven to the very edge of the rock and forced to jump down. But, strange to relate, only one of these men was killed. The others fell into a heap of fine sand, which the wind had piled up against the base of the great rock.

These men were promptly rescued by their comrades, who, knowing this attempt would be followed by a general attack upon all the missions, hastened back to warn Oñate of his peril. After taking immediate measures to protect the priests, Oñate sent a force of seventy men, under Zaldivar's brother, to punish the people of Acoma.

The Indians, warned of the Spaniards' coming, closely guarded their rocky staircases. When the second Zaldivar summoned them to surrender, they mocked him, bade their medicine men curse him, and flung showers of arrows and stones down upon him. The

Spaniards, unable to reach their foes, were obliged to take refuge under the overhanging rock to escape the missiles hurled down upon them.

All night long they heard the shrieks of the Indians. They were holding a monster war dance overhead, and fiercely illustrating the tortures they meant to make the Spaniards suffer the next day. This prospect, however, did not frighten Zaldivar's brave men, and while their foes shouted and danced, they made a clever plan to surprise the city.

Early the next day, Zaldivar and part of his force pretended to storm the north side of the rock. But while they were thus engaging the attention of the Indians, twelve of their number slowly crawled up a neighboring pinnacle of rock, dragging a small cannon after them. No one noticed what they were doing, and it was only when the cannon was in place, and the first stone ball came crashing into the adobe houses, that the Indians perceived their danger.

The rock upon which the Spaniards had planted their cannon was on a level with Acoma, separated from it by a chasm only a few feet wide but about three hundred feet deep. From this point the Spaniards shot ball after ball into the town. When night came on, they crept down again, cut several trees, dragged the trunks up to the top of their rock, and at dawn flung one of them across the abyss.

In spite of a hail of stones and arrows hurled by the Indians, twelve Spaniards rushed boldly across this dizzy bridge before the log was accidentally jerked out of place by one of their number. Cut off from their companions, and unable to retreat, these brave men were now in great danger, for they had to face all those raging savages alone.

Seeing their peril, one of their comrades drew back as far as he could on the outlying rock, and rushing forward took a flying leap across the chasm! By great good fortune he landed safely on the other side, drew the log into place once more, and thus enabled the other Spaniards to cross with their cannon.

One house after another was now battered down, and at the end of three days' hard fighting the Spaniards were complete masters of the Sky City of Acoma. But they soon left it, and many years later, when Fray Ramirez (rah-me´reth), a Spanish priest, came thither and began climbing the staircase, the Indians tried to keep him away by flinging a shower of stones down upon him.

Spanish priests, however, were ready to risk everything for the sake of their religion, so Fray Ramirez calmly continued to climb up. In the general excitement a little Indian girl drew too near to the edge of the rock, and, losing her balance, fell over! Although her people fancied she had fallen to the ground and been killed, she had only dropped to a narrow ledge, where they could not see her. Fray Ramirez, looking upward, saw the accident. Climbing carefully along the ledge, he picked up the little maiden, and soon reappeared on the staircase, carrying her on his shoulder.

The Indians, believing the child dead, now cried out that this was a miracle, and suddenly ceased throwing stones. When the priest reached the plateau they ran to meet him, listened quietly to his teachings, and even built a church in Acoma under his directions. And it is in memory of his coming among them that the stone stairway of Acoma is still known as the "Path of the Father."

XXI. AROUND THE WORLD.

After the voyages of the Cabots in 1497-1498, the English for some time took little interest in the New World. But in the middle of the sixteenth century several noted seamen visited America. One of these men was Hawkins, who brought over from Africa a cargo of negroes. He sold these as slaves to the Spaniards in the West Indies.

Until then prisoners of war had often been sold as slaves, and the Indians on the newly discovered islands had, as we have seen, found cruel taskmasters in the colonists. But as these savages were not used to hard work, they soon died.

Hawkins fancied he was doing a very wise thing in bringing negroes over from Africa to replace them. Indeed, he was so proud of this idea that he had a slave painted on his coat of arms, and said, like Columbus, that it was much better for the negroes to be slaves among Christians than free among heathens.

It was thus that the negro slave trade began, and for two hundred and fifty years slave ships plied to and fro across the Atlantic Ocean, bringing over countless colored people, who were sold first to the Spaniards and later to the Americans.

The English were so anxious to discover a northwest passage to India (that is, a way to sail through or around the northern part of America) that they sent Frob´ish-er out to search for it in 1576. He sailed northward until he came to the bay which still bears his name. He landed there, and, to his delight, found some yellow ore, which he carried home. This was what is now known as fool's gold, or pyrites; but the English, thinking it was real gold, quickly sent out a ship to bring home a whole cargo of the worthless stuff.

Some time after this visit of Frobisher's, Da´vis sailed still farther north, only to be driven back by the ice in the strait which still bears his name. Although he did not know it, Davis had discovered the entrance to the long-sought northwest passage; but it could never be used to reach Asia, as people hoped, on account of the great icebergs which block it up nearly all the year.

Another great English seaman of this time was Francis Drake, who first sailed with the slave trader Hawkins. When he came to the Spanish settlements in the West Indies and Mexico, and saw how much gold was shipped to Spain, he wanted to get some of it for his country, too. He therefore set out with several vessels, and although war had not yet been declared between England and Spain, he boldly attacked the Spanish colonies and ships, and secured much booty.

When war broke out Drake became more daring than ever, and running unexpectedly into the Spanish ports, he began plundering. Then, setting fire to the shipping, he sailed off again, after thus "singeing the King of Spain's beard," as he called it. During one of his many journeys, Drake landed on the Isthmus of Panama, where, climbing the mountains, he was the first Englishman to behold the Pacific Ocean, about fifty years after it had been seen by Balboa.

In the course of his piratical expeditions Drake sailed through the Strait of Magellan into the Pacific Ocean, and, after securing much booty from the Spaniards in Peru, coasted about until he came to the Californian bay which still bears his name. He called this part of the country New Al´bi-on, and made such friends with the Indians there that they invited him to stay and be their king.

But Drake was anxious to carry his treasures home; and as he knew a Spanish fleet was lying in wait for him near the Strait of Magellan, he boldly crossed the Pacific, and went back by way of the Cape of Good Hope. He was thus, as he said, the first Englishman who "plowed a furrow around the globe." Queen E-liz´a-beth was so proud of this fact that she knighted Drake on board of his own ship, the *Pelican*, and graciously accepted all the stolen jewels he gave her (1580).

The Pelican Chair.

The *Pelican* was carefully preserved for about one hundred years, and when it fell to pieces a chair was made from its timbers, and given to the Oxford University, where it can still be seen. As for Drake, he lived to continue his journeys some time longer, and to take part in the great naval battle against the Spanish Ar-ma´da; and he finally perished while on his way to make an attack on the West Indies.

XXII. NOTHING BUT SMOKE.

The greatest of all the English seamen of this time was Sir Walter Raleigh (raw´ly). A poet, philosopher, historian, courtier, and colonizer, Raleigh was also a favorite of Queen Elizabeth. We are told that he won this lady's approval by once spreading his new cloak on the ground so that she might pass dry-shod over a muddy spot.

Raleigh's great ambition was to "plant an English nation in America." He and his half-brother, Sir Humphrey Gil´bert, therefore obtained Elizabeth's permission to start a colony in any part of the New World not yet occupied by any other Christian power. Then Gilbert started across the Atlantic with several ships and took possession of Newfoundland. While cruising near there, one of his vessels was wrecked.

On his return voyage his little fleet was overtaken by a storm. Gilbert was on a leaky vessel, but as the other ships were not large enough to contain all his men, he refused to leave it for a safer one. When they told him that he was in great danger, he quietly answered, "Heaven is as near by water as by land," and calmly went on reading his Bible. The storm increased. All at once the other boats missed the light of Gilbert's ship! They peered anxiously out into the darkness, but all in vain, for the vessel had sunk with its brave captain and all its crew.

Raleigh and Queen Elizabeth.

Undaunted by this first failure, Raleigh soon sent out a new expedition. It brought back such favorable reports of the coast farther south that Raleigh named the country Virgin´i-a, in honor of Elizabeth, the virgin (or unmarried) queen, who gave him a grant of land there.

Among other strange things, Raleigh's explorers brought back potatoes, which had never yet been seen in England. Raleigh planted these on his estate in Ireland, where people were at first afraid to eat them, lest they should be poisonous. Before long, however, potatoes became so common that they have been the chief food of the Irish peasants for many a year.

The first colony established by Raleigh, on Ro-a-noke´ Island, in what is now North Carolina, suffered many hardships. The people were so discouraged by the time Drake came to visit them, that they persuaded him to carry them back to England. Then a second colony was started on the same spot, which thus became the home of the first little English baby born in our country. She was called Virginia, in honor of her birthplace.

A war with Spain prevented Raleigh's sending supplies to this colony for several years, and when the grandfather of the first English-American child finally visited Roanoke, little Virginia had vanished, as well as all the rest of the colonists. No one has ever known what became of them, but it is supposed that they were all killed by the Indians. The only trace ever found was one word carved on a big tree, the name of the neighboring village of Croa-tan´.

These ventures, and his many journeys, made Raleigh so poor that he finally had to give up all his rights to the land.

As we have seen, Raleigh was a great favorite of the queen, therefore many stories are told about him. For instance, it is related that he was the first Englishman to use tobacco, which the Indians said "cured being tired." One day, when Raleigh was smoking in his room, a new servant came in with a pitcher of water. Seeing smoke come out of his master's mouth and nose, the man fancied that Raleigh was on fire, and hastily upset the water on his head to put out the flames!

We are also told that Raleigh taught Queen Elizabeth how to smoke, and that they two enjoyed many a pipe together. On one occasion Raleigh made a bet with the queen that he could tell the exact weight of the smoke from her pipe. First he carefully weighed the tobacco she put in her pipe; then, when she was through smoking, he weighed the ashes, and won his wager by telling her that the difference in weight between tobacco and ashes was that of the smoke! Elizabeth paid the money cheerfully, but remarked that, while she had often heard of turning gold into smoke, he was the first who had turned smoke into gold.

About twenty years after Raleigh founded his first colony, another English seaman, named Gos´nold, decided that it was very foolish to take the roundabout way by Iceland or the Azores Islands to reach America. He therefore boldly steered straight across the Atlantic, thus shortening the trip by about one thousand miles.

The first land he saw he named Cape Cod, because he found so many codfish there. Soon after he stopped on Cut´ty-hunk Island, near the coast, where he built a house. Then, after securing a cargo of sassafras, which was at that time used as a medicine for almost every disease, Gosnold sailed home, leaving his house tenantless.

XXIII. SMITH'S ADVENTURES.

Sir Walter Raleigh was in favor as long as Elizabeth lived, but when she died he was accused of treason and put in prison by James I. While in his cell this brave man wrote a history of the world for young Prince Henry, who often visited him, and longed to free him. He once said: "Only such a king as my father would keep such a bird in such a cage." The same monarch finally ordered Raleigh to be put to death. Mounting the scaffold, the prisoner asked to see the ax, and, running his finger along its edge to test its keenness, said: "This is a sharp medicine, but a cure for all evils."

Before going to prison Raleigh had given up all his claims in America to English merchants. They formed two bodies, the London Company and the Plym´oŭth Company, and persuaded the king to give each of them a piece of land in North America one hundred miles square.

This matter being decided, the London Company sent out a shipload of settlers, who, in 1607, sailed into Ches´a-peake Bay. They called the capes on either side Charles and

Henry, in honor of the two princes; then, passing up a river, they landed on a marshy cape, where they founded the first lasting English colony in the United States. River and town were both named after King James, who had selected their officers and made their laws.

The James'town colonists were nearly all gentlemen, who had come without their families because they intended to stay only long enough to get rich. As there were only four carpenters among them, these men were kept very busy. But, instead of building comfortable houses, and plowing and sowing, the rest of the settlers spent all their time looking for gold. The result was that their supplies gave out, and as the Indians were unfriendly and would not give them food, they were soon in danger of starving. Besides, Jamestown was on low, damp ground, and the water was so bad that the ill-fed people suffered from malaria, and about half of them died.

Among the Englishmen who had come to Virginia there was Captain John Smith. This man had been a soldier, had traveled a great deal, and had visited France, Italy, and E'gypt.

We are told that while he was on his way to Egypt a great storm once overtook his ship. The pilgrims on the vessel cried out that there must be a wrongdoer, or a Jonah, among them, and in their terror proposed to draw lots. Finding out thus that Smith was the guilty person, they hastily pitched him overboard. But although there was no whale to swallow him, Smith managed to swim ashore, and some time later, longing for more adventures, he went to fight in Hun'ga-ry.

Here he declared that the teachings of Christ were far better than those of Mo-ham'med, and offered to prove it by fighting three Turks. He killed them all, but, being wounded, was soon made a prisoner and sold as a slave. One day, when Smith was threshing in the field, his cruel taskmaster beat him severely, although he had done nothing wrong. Indignant at this unjust treatment, Smith suddenly raised his flail, and struck the Turk such a hard blow that the man fell to the ground dead.

Seeing a chance to escape, Smith now quickly exchanged clothes with the dead man, hid the latter's body under the straw, filled a bag with corn, and jumping on a horse rode rapidly away across the plains. After many days of hard riding, he came to a place where his chains were struck off, and thence continued his journey home.

After several other journeys and adventures, Smith joined the newly formed London Company, proposing to go out himself with the colonists. On the way to Virginia he was falsely accused of crime, and nearly hanged; but when he reached land his innocence was proved, and he soon became the leading spirit of Jamestown.

Through all the sickness and famine Smith alone seemed brave and strong. Hoping to secure food for the colonists, he once set out to find the Indians and trade with them for corn. But at the approach of the English, we are told that the savages ran away in such haste that they left their dinner on the fire. The colonists, drawing near, saw that the Indians had been roasting oysters, and, tasting them for the first time in their lives, were delighted to discover a new and delicious kind of food. After shooting a few turkeys, the English overtook these Indians, from whom they managed to get quite a supply of corn in exchange for trinkets and a copper kettle.

In another expedition Captain Smith was surprised by the Indians while he stood in a marsh, picking berries. He seized one of the savages and held him fast, using him as a shield against the arrows of the rest until surrounded and made a prisoner.

Instead of showing anger or resisting, Smith now followed his captors quietly, allowing them to touch and examine him as much as they pleased. He also tried to interest them by showing them his compass and explaining its use. Besides, he made friends with the Indian children and whittled playthings for them. All the prettiest ones, however, were set aside for Po-ca-hon´tas, the twelve-year-old daughter of the Indian chief Pow-ha-tan´; and it seems she was specially pleased with the wooden doll he made for her.

Smith and Pocahontas.

We are told that Pocahontas soon grew very fond of Captain Smith, and that when the Indians once tried to kill him, she stood between him and their raised tomahawks, pleading so hard for his life that her father declared the white man should not be slain. But this story is also told of several other explorers, and we do not know if it is quite true.

XXIV. THE JAMESTOWN MEN.

After several weeks of captivity Captain Smith bargained with the Indians to set him free, in exchange for a certain number of trinkets and one of the bright brass cannons they had seen at Jamestown. This settled, he wrote a letter to the colonists, telling them what trinkets they were to give the bearers, and warning them to be sure to shoot off the cannon in the Indians' presence, so that they should not dare carry it off.

Having finished his letter, Smith gave it to his captors, bidding them take it to Jamestown. He added that it would tell the English what they wanted, and that they would hear the big noise which came out of the bright log (cannon) they coveted. All this, of course, seemed very mysterious to people who did not know how to write, so they set out for Jamestown full of curiosity.

When they saw that the white men, after looking at the letter, gave them all the trinkets they had bargained for, they were amazed. Then they tried to lift the bright log, and were surprised at its weight. Motioning them aside, the colonists next shot off the cannon. The loud noise, and the fact that the cannon ball splintered a good-sized tree, filled the Indians with such terror that, as Smith had foreseen, they refused to touch it again. When they got back to their camp they let Captain Smith go, and he bade a friendly good-by to the red men, from whom he had learned all he could during his short sojourn in their midst.

Free once more, Captain Smith used all his energies to get enough grain for his friends; but had it not been for the Indian girl Pocahontas the colonists would probably have starved to death. Several times, in the course of that first hard winter, she brought them game and corn, and, thanks to her pleading, her father Powhatan became quite friendly, and supplied their most pressing needs.

In 1608 more colonists came over to Jamestown in search of gold; but they, too, were gentlemen, and intended to remain only a short time. They unfortunately discovered some pyrites, and in spite of all Captain Smith could say, there was "no talk, no hope, no work, but dig gold, wash gold, refine gold, load gold." The result was that the vessel in which they had come was sent home laden with worthless dirt, instead of carrying a cargo of lumber, sassafras, or furs, which could have been sold in England for considerable money.

The only man who did not share this thirst for gold was Captain Smith. He continued his explorations, and made a complete map of Chesapeake Bay to send back to England. Then, the governor having sailed away with the fool's gold, and the others having proved bad managers, Smith was soon chosen to be head of the colony.

He began his work by making a few very strict rules, which all the colonists had to obey. The fine English gentlemen, who had spent their time playing bowls in the streets of Jamestown, priding themselves upon never having done any labor, were now told that if they would not work they should not eat.

To stop the constant swearing in which these men freely indulged, Captain Smith next ordered that a canful of cold water should be poured down any offender's sleeve. This soon put an end to profanity, and by the time a third set of colonists reached Jamestown it was quite an orderly community.

Crowning Powhatan.

Two women came out with these last-mentioned settlers to make real homes in Jamestown, the first English city in what is now the United States. The same ship also brought over presents from King James to the Indian King Powhatan. These were a bed, basin and pitcher, a coat trimmed with gold lace, and a crown.

Powhatan was therefore solemnly invited to Jamestown, to receive these gifts and be crowned. The Indian chief was greatly pleased with his fine red coat. But no one could make him understand that he must kneel to receive his crown. Finally, in despair, the colonists standing on either side of him leaned so heavily upon his shoulders that they forced him to bend the knee before the governor, who quickly crowned him.

To the savages' great delight, drums were loudly beaten in honor of King Powhatan, but when the cannon was shot off, too, the newly crowned king of Virginia was so amazed that he almost fell over backward. When he had recovered from his fright Powhatan gave the governor his old moccasins, or shoes, and a tattered and dirty robe of raccoon skins, telling him to send them to King James in return for his gifts!

XXV. SMITH WOUNDED.

The last Jamestown settlers brought over letters in which the English merchants asked for gold, and urged the colonists to make diligent search for a passage to India, where so much money could be made by trading for silks, pearls, and spices. In obedience to these orders, a new excursion was tried, but of course no such passage was ever found on the coast of Virginia.

When the ships went back to England, Smith sent a letter to the company, begging them to send out farmers, carpenters, blacksmiths, masons, and men to cut down trees, rather than so many fine gentlemen who did not know how to work.

Then, as soon as the ships had gone, Captain Smith set all the colonists to work building houses, planting corn, and working hard in many ways, so as to supply their daily needs. He also ordered that the Indians should be treated kindly. But the settlers, thinking they knew better than he, refused to work, and treated the Indians so unjustly that they secretly planned to kill all the English.

We are told that this plot was overheard by Pocahontas. She ran through the forest all alone, one dark night, and, coming to Jamestown, secretly told Captain Smith of his peril. He was so grateful to Pocahontas for her warning that he wanted to give her a present; but she refused it, saying that if her people saw it they would suspect she had betrayed them.

By Captain Smith's wise measures, the Indians were awed into good behavior, and for a time Jamestown was safe. But, unfortunately, a terrible accident soon happened to the brave man who had been the life of the colony. A gun, shot off by accident, set fire to the powder in a boat where Smith lay asleep. He was badly wounded, and would have been burned to death had he not had the presence of mind to roll out of the boat into the water.

There were no good doctors in Jamestown, and as the wound in his thigh did not heal, Captain Smith sailed back to England in the next vessel, never to visit Jamestown again. But when quite cured he explored the northeast coast of our country, and drew a good map of it, calling that part of America New England. It was in reward for this service that the king gave him the title of "Admiral of New England." Being now too old to continue his journeys any longer, Smith spent the rest of his life in writing an account of his travels and of the founding of Jamestown.

Some people say that Captain Smith, like many sailors, was so fond of spinning yarns that he did not always tell the exact truth. He cannot have been a bad man, however, for when he died, those who had gone out to Jamestown with him said that he hated baseness, laziness, pride, and falsehood; that he never sent any one into a danger he was not ready to share; that he was strictly honest in all his dealings; and that he loved actions more than words; and he was honored and mourned by all. Brave Captain Smith was buried in London, where his friends placed this inscription over his grave: "Here lies one conquered, that hath conquered kings."

After Captain Smith left them, the Jamestown colonists became idler than ever, and treated the Indians so unkindly that even Pocahontas refused to visit them any more. The result was that they could not buy any corn, and as they had no crops of their own, they had so little food, when winter came, that only sixty out of about six hundred colonists managed to live.

This terrible winter in Jamestown is known in history as "Starvation Time;" and some people say that the settlers became so desperate from hunger that they actually turned cannibals. Their sufferings were so great that those who survived determined to go home in the spring. So they put their scant stock of provisions on board their ships, and prepared to sail.

But before leaving they wanted to set fire to the houses they had built, and destroy the place where "none had enjoyed one happy day." The governor, however, refused to let them do this. To make sure his orders should not be disobeyed, he embarked last, after seeing that all was safe.

The little band of discouraged settlers now sailed slowly down the James River. But on reaching its mouth, they were overjoyed to meet three ships coming from England, with a stock of provisions and many new colonists. They therefore turned around and went back to Jamestown, where, you may be sure, they were very thankful to find their houses still standing and all ready to receive them.

XXVI. THE VISIT OF POCAHONTAS TO ENGLAND.

A new governor, named Dale, now took charge of the Jamestown colony, and seeing that the colonists were lazy and indifferent, he tried to find out the cause. He soon discovered that the workers thought it unjust that they should have to feed the lazy, for the rule had been that all supplies should go into a common storehouse, and that each man should receive an equal share.

As the company had in 1609 received a new charter from the king, granting them land for four hundred miles along the coast, and thence "up into the land throughout from sea to sea, west and northwest," they were very anxious that the Jamestown colony should thrive. Dale, therefore, now said that each man should work for himself only. The result was that those who were willing to labor were soon very comfortable, while the lazy colonists became poorer and poorer. Still, seeing that they must work or starve, the idlers now did enough to keep themselves alive.

Other laws were made at the same time, and it was decided that those who disobeyed them should have their tongues pierced with a red-hot iron. From this time on Jamestown prospered; more colonists came, grain became plentiful, and instead of digging for gold, the settlers planted tobacco to sell in England.

The English had by this time learned to like tobacco, although King James disapproved so strongly of smoking that he wrote a book called "A Counterblast to Tobacco." In fact, the use of this weed was so general that the colonists, finding they could get about seventy-five cents a pound for it, raised all they could, thus following the example set by John Rolfe, one of their number.

Four years after Captain Smith left the Jamestown colony, the English captain Ar´gall, remembering how useful Pocahontas had been, determined to capture her. Hearing that she was with a neighboring tribe, he bargained with the chief to lure her on board his vessel and leave her there.

The chief consented, and walked off in triumph with his reward,—a shiny copper kettle,—leaving Pocahontas in the hands of Captain Argall. He took her to Jamestown, where she was kindly treated. John Rolfe converted the young prisoner, and made her his wife as soon as she had been baptized. Powhatan and many of his tribe were invited to this wedding, the first between an Englishman and an Indian girl. Of course it was a great event in the colony, so when the next ship went back to England it carried this piece of news to court.

Marriage of Pocahontas.

When the king heard it he was greatly displeased, for he fancied that, after marrying the daughter of the King of Virginia, Rolfe might want to rule over the country. But Rolfe wished nothing of the kind, and after growing tobacco for a while, he took his Indian wife to England.

To please Captain Smith, the queen welcomed Pocahontas kindly. She appeared at court in fashionable English clothes,—which must have seemed very uncomfortable to an Indian,—and was presented as the "Lady Rebecca," for since her baptism her name had been changed. Pocahontas spent a few months in England, and she had just started to return to Virginia, when she was taken ill and died. But she left a little son, who lived to grow up and became the ancestor of several noted families in Virginia.

Wives for the Virginians.

The colonists soon found tobacco so profitable that they planted it even in the streets of Jamestown, and used it for money. Instead of saying a thing was worth so many dollars, as we do now, they said it was worth so many pounds of tobacco. They rapidly grew rich, and as they no longer feared starvation, all longed to have wives to make them comfortable.

They therefore wrote to England, asking that women should be sent out to them, offering to give from one hundred to one hundred and fifty pounds of tobacco to pay for their passage. The next ship, therefore, brought over a cargo of young women, and the men who wanted wives rushed down to the wharf, and wooed them so eagerly that there were soon many happy homes in Virginia.

As tobacco crops rapidly exhaust the soil, the colonists occupied more and more land, settling generally near a stream, so that vessels could come and load at their private docks. And because tobacco is planted, and not sown, their lands were called plantations, a name still used in the South for any large farm. Some people, however, say the name was given to any settlement planted in a new place.

To make sure they would always have a good government, the Virginia planters, who in 1619 had eleven settlements, or boroughs, chose two men from each borough to sit in a House of Bur′ges-ses at Jamestown. These burgesses helped to make a set of laws, called the "Great Charter." The fact that the colonists now had a share in ruling themselves, made them take special pride in their new homes, although they still spoke lovingly of England as the "mother country."

Strange to relate, the same year that the Virginia colonists claimed their right as freemen to help govern themselves, a Dutch ship brought twenty negroes to Jamestown, and sold them as slaves. But although these were the first colored people in our country, they were not the first or only slaves, for the king had already sent out a number of convicts and homeless children to serve the colonists.

There was always a great difference between white and colored slaves. White men were sold only for a certain length of time, after which they again became free; but the negroes were sold for good and all, and they and their children were to be slaves forever.

XXVII. HUDSON AND THE INDIANS.

While the English were gaining ground in Virginia, the other nations were not idle. The Spaniards, as we have seen, had settled in Florida and New Mexico, and, in the latter place especially, their priests started several mission stations.

This was very dangerous work, because they often had to go alone among the Indians, who at times rose up against them and even tortured them to death. But these priests were quite ready to die for the sake of their religion, and although in the course of the next one hundred years more than forty were murdered, others were always ready to take their places.

After many failures the Spaniards finally made friends with and converted most of the Pueb′lo Indians, who learned to live on peaceable terms with the white men, as they still do to-day. In fact, although they had but one small town, Santa Fé, the Spaniards had many missions and eleven churches in New Mexico before the Jamestown colonists first sat in the House of Burgesses.

The French Huguenots, as already said, tried to make a settlement in the southern part of our country, but had been murdered by their Spanish neighbors. Next, some Frenchmen tried to settle in Maine, but soon gave up the attempt. Their first lasting settlement was therefore made in 1604, at Port. Royal in A-ca′di-a, where they at first suffered much, but afterwards prospered greatly and had comfortable homes.

The Dutch, living near the ocean, were great seamen and traders, so you will not be surprised to hear that they, too, sent ships across the Atlantic before long. One of these vessels, the *Half-Moon*, under Henry Hudson, came over here to look for the northwest passage. Sailing along the New England coast, and thence southward, Hudson entered

Del'a-ware and New York bays. He also sailed up a great stream, then called the North River, but now generally known as the Hudson (1609).

At first Hudson thought this broad river must be the long-sought road to India, because at high tide the water was salt many miles upstream. But sailing on, he finally discovered that it was a river, which he explored to the point where Al'ba-ny now stands. It was in September, the weather was beautiful, and Hudson and his crew were in raptures over the lovely views. The coming of this vessel created a great sensation among the Indians, who rushed to the edge of the water to see the "great white bird." They called the *Half-Moon* a bird on account of its spreading sails.

Hudson on the River.

Hudson traded with the natives for tobacco and furs, and once when they tried to steal some of his trinkets he gave them a terrible fright by shooting off his cannon. On his return he landed on Man-hat'tan Island, where the Indians gave him a feast, breaking their arrows to show he need fear no treachery on their part.

We are told that, in exchange for their hospitality, Hudson offered the savages some rum to drink. They looked at it, and smelled it, but passed it on without tasting it. Finally the bottle came to an Indian who was somewhat bolder than the rest, or who feared to offend the white man. He drank a great deal of the liquor, but he had no sooner done so than he fell down senseless, and all his companions thought he was dead.

After a few hours, however, the Indian awoke from his drunken sleep, to remark that the Dutchman had the strongest water he had ever tasted. The other savages were now all eager to try the "fire water" too; and, having drunk it once, they took such a fancy to it that before long they were ready to give all they had in exchange for more. But, as you will see, this fire water was to do them a great deal of harm.

On his way home Hudson stopped in England, where they kept him a prisoner, saying an Englishman ought to make discoveries only for the good of his own country. But Hudson managed to send a description of his journey to Holland, and he then reported that he had visited "as beautiful a land as one can tread upon." Hearing from him also that great bargains in furs could be made with the Indians, Dutch merchants soon sent out vessels to establish trading stations near Albany and on Manhattan Island.

While the Dutch were thus bartering, Hudson, set free, started out on a voyage for England. Sailing farther north, in search of a passage to India, he came, in 1611, to the bay which still bears his name. Here his crew suffered so much from the cold climate that, in their anger against their captain, they put him, his son, and seven sick men in a boat, and cut them adrift. The ship came back to Europe in safety, but nothing more was ever heard of Hudson or the unfortunate sailors with him.

The Dutch soon built Fort Orange on the Hudson, near Albany, Fort Nas'sau on the Delaware, and, later, a fort on Manhattan Island. Here, in 1614, they founded the colony later called New Am'ster-dam, on the very spot where a shipwrecked captain had built the first Dutch-American vessel about one year before. Little by little the Dutch now took possession of the land along the Hudson River and New York Bay. They built comfortable houses of bricks brought over from Holland, and before long had many thrifty farms in what they called the New Neth'er-lands.

XXVIII. THE MAYFLOWER.

While the Spaniards were settling in Florida and New Mexico, the French in Acadia, and the Dutch in the New Netherlands, the English, as we have seen, had also been busy. In Virginia they had founded Jamestown, and Gosnold and John Smith had visited and named several places in New England, such as Cape Cod and the Charles River.

During the next few years several attempts were made to found a colony in New England, but all failed. Still, although no real settlements were made, English fishing vessels were often seen along the coast, where codfish could easily be caught and dried. The captain of one of these fishing boats is said to have captured twenty-four Indians, whom he carried off to sell as slaves. Among these savages was one named Squan'to. He was taken first to Spain and then to England before he was shipped back to his native land.

When poor Squanto finally reached the New England shores once more he found everything sadly changed. During his absence a terrible plague had broken out and swept away nearly all his tribe. Wigwams, fields, hunting and fishing grounds were now deserted, and the few Indians who had escaped death had gone to live elsewhere. Squanto therefore joined another tribe, to whom he soon proved very useful, for he had learned enough English to serve as interpreter between them and the fishermen.

Nowadays people can be of any religion they choose, but in the beginning of the seventeenth century every one was expected to practice the religion of the country in which he lived. After following the Roman Catholic religion for about nine centuries, the English, in the middle of the sixteenth century, suddenly decided that England should have a church of her own. Their king, Henry VIII., said that while the pope was head of the Roman Catholic Church, he would henceforth be head of the An'gli-can or English Church. He added that all his subjects would have to attend the services of that church, and pay a tax to him for its support, just as they had done to the pope.

Although there were a great many people quite willing to do this, others said that nothing would induce them to give up the Roman Catholic religion. These people were very firm, and although the king tried to force them to change their religion, many of them bravely died rather than do what they considered wrong.

At first there were only Roman Catholics and Anglicans in England. But after a time some of the Anglicans said that they wanted a plainer and *purer* religion. They repeated this so often that before long they were known all over England as the Pu'ri-tans. Next, some of the Puritans refused to go to the Anglican Church at all, or to pay for its support, and because they did this they were treated just as unkindly as the Roman Catholics.

Those Puritans who separated themselves from their brethren and refused to go to the Anglican Church were soon called Sep'a-ra-tists. They were held in great contempt, and persecuted by all those who did not believe exactly as they did. After standing this for several years, some of them left England in 1607, and after many trials founded a Separatist colony at Leȳ'den in Holland.

Here they had to work very hard to make a living; and although they tried to keep their children apart from the rest of the people, they soon saw that the boys and girls were learning the Dutch language and ways so rapidly that before long they would cease to be English. The Separatists therefore began to wonder where they could go so their children would hear nothing but the English language, have no dealings with people of a different religion, and still have a fair chance to make a living.

They finally decided to go to the New World, and sent to ask King James's permission to found a colony in a place where, while remaining his faithful subjects, they could worship as they pleased. James allowed them to go to America, but refused to give them a paper granting all the rights they wished. Still, as the Separatists knew that the king was as likely to break a written promise as a verbal one, they made up their minds to run the risk.

Too poor to hire vessels to carry them and their goods across the ocean, the Separatists borrowed the necessary money from English speculators, promising that all their earnings for the next seven years should be equally divided between the merchants and the colonists. Then, hearing that none but Church of England people would be received in Virginia, they decided to settle in the land Hudson had described so favorably.

As the Separatists were about to set out on a long pilgrimage, or journey, for the sake of their religion, they took the name of Pilgrims. The youngest and strongest among them were to go out first, under the guidance of one of their teachers, Elder Brewster. But all the old and feeble members were to remain in Holland a little longer, in charge of their minister, Mr. Rob´in-son. After a last feast together, and a solemn parting prayer, the Pilgrims received their pastor's blessing, said good-by to their friends, and embarked on the *Speedwell* at Delfs-ha´ven. The spot whence they started is now marked by a monument commemorating their departure, and from there Robinson prayerfully watched them until they were out of sight. Although their vessel was old and leaky, the Pilgrims reached South-amp´ton safely. Here they found friends waiting for them, and all ready to sail in the *Mayflower*. After a short delay both vessels set out together; but they soon had to put back, because the *Speedwell* proved unsafe. Leaving it at Plymouth, one hundred and two of the most determined Pilgrims embarked on the *Mayflower*, which set out alone to cross the Atlantic Ocean (1620).

The Mayflower.

In those times all travel, whether by land or sea, was very slow. It was therefore only after sixty-three days that the *Mayflower*, driven out of its course by a storm, reached Cape Cod Bay. Thus, you see, it came to the shores of New England instead of New York or New Jersey. During that long and tempestuous journey one of the passengers died; but as one little baby was born on the ship, the Pilgrims still numbered one hundred and two souls.

XXIX. PLYMOUTH ROCK.

The season was so far advanced when the Pilgrims reached our northeast coast, and the seas were so rough, that the captain of the *Mayflower* said it would not be safe to go any farther. So the Pilgrims, who were tired of the ship and eager to begin building their new homes, decided to settle in New England. Before they left the ship, however, the men assembled in the little cabin to draw up a paper, in which they pledged themselves to be true to their country, king, and religion, and to obey any laws made for the good of the colony. Then they elected John Carver, one of their number, as governor for one year, and named Miles Stand´ish, an old soldier, their captain.

The First Wash Day.

While the women hastened ashore to wash their linen, Standish and his little band of Pilgrim soldiers began to explore the coast to find the best spot for their settlement. For a few days they tramped up and down on Cape Cod, once only catching a glimpse of an

Indian and a dog. But finally they came to a ruined wigwam, where they saw a copper kettle. This showed them that Europeans had been there before. Soon after they found some buried corn, and carried it off, intending to pay the owners for it later.

About three weeks after this, some Pilgrims and seamen took a boat and sailed off to make a more extensive exploration of the coast. After going a long distance they landed, and as they walked along they were surprised to find so many graves, for they did not know then that the plague had raged there two years before. Early one day, after spending an uncomfortable night out of doors, and saying their morning prayers, the explorers were startled by a terrible Indian war whoop, and a flight of arrows fell all around them.

But Miles Standish was so brave a man that he made his men stand firm and drive the Indians away. The Indians had attacked the party only because they fancied that the Pilgrims had come to steal Indians, as the fishermen had done several times before.

The Pilgrims now continued their explorations in the midst of a driving snowstorm. Their rudder broke, and they had to steer with their oars. Finally they were driven ashore, where they kindled a fire, spending Sunday in prayer and praise, and resuming their journey only on Monday morning.

On December 21 or 22 they again ran ashore, landing on a rock, since called "the stepping-stone of New England," and now carefully preserved and known as "Plymouth Rock." The land around seemed so favorable that they decided to plant their colony here, naming it Plymouth, in honor of the last English town they had seen before leaving old England.

As the landing of the Pilgrim fathers is one of the great events of our history, the anniversary of their coming is still kept in New England and elsewhere, and is known as "Forefathers' Day."

Landing on Plymouth Rock.

While Standish and his men were busy exploring, the *Mayflower* rode at anchor, and its inmates barely escaped a horrible death. One of the colonists, named Bil´ling-ton, having, gone into the cabin to get powder, carelessly left the barrel open. His boy, a mischievous youngster, crept into the cabin unseen, and began playing with a gun. Of course it went off unexpectedly, and the child came very near setting fire to the powder in the barrel, and thus blowing up the *Mayflower* and all on board.

As soon as Standish had made his report, the anchor was raised, and four days later the Pilgrims landed on Plymouth Rock. The first woman to set foot upon it, we are told, was a Puritan maiden. Soon all the settlers were very busy building a storehouse for their provisions, and homes for themselves.

The men, exposed to the bad weather, caught such heavy colds that before long all were ill, and when the storehouse and a log hut were finished, both had to serve as hospitals for the sick. In spite of an unusually mild winter, the colonists found their close quarters on the *Mayflower* and in damp log houses so uncomfortable that they suffered greatly.

At one time all but seven were seriously ill, and in the course of the winter nearly half of their number perished. Grave after grave was dug in the frozen ground, but the Pilgrims dared not mark them in any way, lest the Indians should discover how many of the white men had died. They were careful about this, because, although they had not seen any, they knew that Indians were lurking near them, for tools left in the woods a few hours had mysteriously vanished.

XXX. THE FIRST AMERICAN THANKSGIVING.

Early in the spring the Pilgrims were startled, one day, by the voice of an Indian saying: "Welcome, Englishmen." Looking up, they saw a savage named Sam´o-set, who had boldly walked into their village to greet them with words learned from English fishermen.

The Pilgrims received Samoset so kindly that he came back on the morrow with Squanto, who told the colonists that the Indian chief Mas´sa-soit wished to make friends with them. A meeting was appointed, and when Massasoit appeared, a few days later, Standish received him. The drums were beaten loudly, and the Pilgrim soldiers gravely escorted the Indian chief to their principal log hut, where Governor Carver was waiting for them.

Here all the choice articles of the Pilgrims had been gathered together to make a fine show, and a rug and green cushion were laid on the floor for Massasoit to sit upon.

After smoking the calumet, or "pipe of peace," together, the Indian chief and the Plymouth governor—with the help of their interpreters—made a treaty, whereby they promised not to harm but to help each other, and to trade in a friendly spirit.

The Indians now walked freely in and out of the village, where they ate and drank so much that the Pilgrims' scant stock of provisions grew rapidly less. Edward Wins´low, one of the Pilgrims, therefore took occasion, on returning Massasoit's visit, to tell him that the Indians were to come to Plymouth only when they bore messages from him. To make sure that the right Indians would always be well treated, Winslow gave Massasoit a ring, which was to serve as passport for his men.

Were you to read Winslow's description of his visit to the Indian chief, you would be greatly amused. Massasoit had no provisions in his wigwam, so he and his guests went to bed hungry. Besides, Winslow and his men had to sleep side by side with the dirty chief and his squaw, and they were so crowded by other Indians that they were very uncomfortable indeed.

In April the *Mayflower* went back to England; but although the Pilgrims had suffered so sorely during the winter, they all wrote brave letters to send home, and not one of them asked to go back. After the *Mayflower* had sailed away Governor Carver fell ill and died, so William Bradford was elected to take his place. This Bradford made so good a ruler that he was elected again and again, and during the next thirty-six years he was head of the colony nearly all the time.

Squanto soon became a great favorite with the Pilgrims. He played with the children, taught the boys to trap game, and told the settlers to plant their corn as soon as the leaves of the white oak were as large as a mouse's ear. He also taught them to put a fat fish in each hill, to serve as manure for the growing grain, because the ground around there was very sandy.

The colonists now worked diligently, making their fields and gardens over the graves of their dead companions, so that no hostile Indians should ever find out how many had died, or dig up their bones. The crops being all planted, the Pilgrims went on building, made friends with nine Indian chiefs, and traded briskly with the savages for furs.

But day by day the stock of provisions brought from England grew less and less, until they finally saw with dismay that it would be entirely exhausted long before their corn was ripe. So they were put on such scant rations that it is said they sometimes had only six grains of corn for a meal! As they were not good hunters or experienced fishermen, they lived almost entirely on shellfish, Elder Brewster piously giving thanks to God for supplying them with "the abundance of the seas and the treasures hid in the sand."

47

Although the winter had been very damp, the summer proved so dry that it soon seemed as if the Pilgrims' crops would perish for want of rain. A day of fasting and prayer was therefore appointed, and for nine hours the Pilgrims besought God to help them. Some Indians, hearing that they were going to pray for rain, watched the sky anxiously, and when it finally clouded over and a gentle rain began to fall, they remarked in awe-struck tones that the God of the white men had evidently heard their prayers.

Ten days of moisture which followed the day of prayer assured a plentiful harvest, which was safely gathered. The Pilgrims were so grateful for this mercy that they set a day in which to give thanks. After a solemn service they held a great feast, to which Massasoit and ninety other Indians were invited.

At this dinner they ate wild turkeys shot by the colonists, venison supplied by the savages, and pies which the Pilgrim mothers made from yellow pumpkins, as they had no apples. During the next three days all the young people indulged in games and athletic sports, in which the Indians also shared. After this "Thanksgiving Day," as the Pilgrims named it, a feast like it was kept every year in New England. This custom gradually spread from there over the whole country, until now the day is observed in all the states of our Union. The President, who appoints the day, generally chooses the last Thursday in November.

The First Thanksgiving Dinner.

XXXI. THE SNAKE SKIN AND THE BULLETS.

As the Pilgrims were just in all their dealings with the Indians, and honestly paid them for the corn taken when they first landed, the natives became quite friendly. They not only brought back the missing tools, but once found and carried home the mischievous Billington boy, who had lost his way in the forest, near the pond which still bears his name.

The Indians felt such respect for the Pilgrims that when Massasoit fell ill he sent for Winslow right away. The latter went to the chief's wigwam, where he found a crowd of Indians eagerly watching the antics of the medicine man, who had come to drive away the chief's disease.

After ordering all the Indians out of the wigwam, Winslow let in some fresh air, cooled the sick Indian's hot brow and hands with clean water, and gave him some medicine. Presently the savage chief asked for chicken broth, which he had once tasted at Plymouth, so Winslow sent a messenger to Plymouth for a fowl. Thanks to Winslow's good nursing,—for fresh air and cleanliness are good doctors,—Massasoit soon recovered, and ever after he was the white men's firm ally.

All the Indians were not friendly, however. Ca-non´i-cus, chief of the Nar-ra-gan´setts, an enemy of Massasoit, hated to see the land occupied by the English, so he soon sent them a rattlesnake's skin full of arrows. Governor Bradford looked at it wonderingly and then asked Squanto what it meant. The Indian said it signified that unless the white men crept away like serpents the Indians would slay them all with their arrows.

Hearing this, Bradford coolly took the arrows out of the skin, stuffed it full of powder and bullets, and silently handed it to the messenger to carry back to Canonicus. The savage glided rapidly away, and gave the skin to Canonicus, who, afraid of the powder, passed it on to another Indian. The snake skin went thus from hand to hand, but was finally sent back to Plymouth, with an offer of friendship. The Indians, seeing that the English governor was not afraid of them, now begged for peace, promising to bury the war hatchet so deep that it could never again be dug up.

The fact is that powder at first seemed a very mysterious thing to the red men. They were afraid of it, but at the same time longed to have some. One Indian is said to have bought powder from a colonist, who gravely told him that if he wanted any more he must plant the black seed. The savage obeyed, but as nothing came up from it, the shrewd Indian declared that he would pay the colonist only when the powder grew!

The Pilgrims, fearing the Indians might attack them, built a log meetinghouse on a hill, and used it as a fort, placing their cannon on its flat roof. This place was also surrounded by a palisade, or great fence of tree trunks, so that it could afford the colonists a safe shelter in time of danger. Generally, however, it served as a meetinghouse, for the Pilgrims were all very religious, and when the drums beat on Sunday morning all came out of their houses and marched in solemn procession to church.

At the door the men stacked their arms, leaving them in charge of a guard, who was to give the alarm at the first sign of danger. In the meetinghouse men and women sat apart, listening to the long prayers and sermons, or slowly singing very sober hymns. The boys sat on the pulpit steps, in full view of the congregation, to make sure they would behave properly.

The sexton, armed with a long stick, rapped the boys on the head if they proved unruly, or poked the men when they fell asleep. But if the girls or women dozed, he gently tickled their cheeks with the foxtail hanging at the other end of the same stick. Sometimes, too, it was he who turned the hourglass when all its sands had run out, for the minister was then only halfway through his two hours' sermon.

In the first fall the colony was increased by the arrival of more Separatists; but it did not really prosper until the settlers bought the shares of the English merchants, and, instead of holding everything in common, began to work each for himself. They were so industrious and thrifty that before long their debts were all paid, and they had comfortable homes and good farms.

The Plymouth people were so strict that they would allow none but church members to vote. Their colony therefore grew very slowly, and at the end of ten years it numbered only about three hundred souls. But other Puritans, who did not believe exactly as the Plymouth colonists, came over to America and founded other colonies along the New England coast.

G. H. Boughton, Artist.

Pilgrims going to Church.

Thus, for instance, the first Mas-sa-chu'setts Bay colonists came over in 1628. As their hope was to convert the Indians, they adopted a seal on which there was an Indian, with the inscription, "Come over and help us." They, too, were very strict. They said, "No idle drone may live among us," and expected every one to work hard. They settled at some distance from Plymouth (map, page 230), in a spot which they called Sa'lem ("Peace"), because they hoped to live and worship there in peace.

The principal man in the Massachusetts Bay colony was John En'di-cott. He felt such intense horror for the Roman Catholic religion that before he had been in America very long, he drew out his sword and cut the cross right out of the English flag, saying that Puritans could not look with respect upon such a popish emblem. Besides, hearing that some English colonists had put up a Maypole on Merry Mount, and danced there, he cut down the pole and scolded the people for indulging in "the folly of amusements."

XXXII. THE BEGINNING OF BOSTON.

Besides Puritans, a few other men came over to New England. Among these was Standish, who, as you know, proved very useful to the Plymouth colony, and a learned man named Black´stone. The latter tried at first to live with the Separatists at Plymouth, but when he saw that they were not willing to let him do as he thought right, and wanted to force him to think just as they did, he boldly said: "I came from England because I did not like the Lord Bishops, but I cannot join with you, because I would not be under the Lord Brethren."

Having spoken thus, Blackstone left the colony, and withdrew to a hill about forty miles up the coast, where he built himself a comfortable house. Here he soon had a fine garden, where he grew the first apples seen in New England; and his cow, wandering around in search of pasture, made the first winding paths through the forest in that part of the country.

Although the Plymouth settlers were, as we have seen, usually on friendly terms with the Indians, there were some worthless settlers where Weymouth (wā´mŭth) now is, who soon quarreled with them (1623). Hearing that the Indians had planned to kill all the whites, Captain Standish and his little force marched over to Weymouth. Though small, he was very brave. He sent for the Indian chiefs, and met them in a log hut. When one of them threatened his life, Standish boldly attacked him. There was a terrible tussle, but the white man finally killed his huge enemy. This act of daring made other Indians respect Standish, whom they called the "big little man."

While Standish was struggling with one Indian, two more were killed by the other white men in the hut, and a few others were slain afterwards. When this news reached Mr. Robinson at Leyden, he sadly cried: "Oh, that they had converted some before they killed any!"

In 1630 the colonists of Massachusetts Bay were reinforced by the arrival of seven hundred newcomers, "the very flower of the English Puritans." Led by John Winthrop, a noble and clever man, some of them came over in a ship which was called the *Lady Arbela*, in honor of a delicate lady on board. But seventy-six days of sea journey proved so trying to this frail woman that she died soon after landing at Salem.

At first the newcomers tried to settle near Charles´town; but they found the drinking water so bad there that they finally went to Trimountain, or Tre´mont ("Three Hills"), where Blackstone had built his house. Not liking to live so near a large colony of Puritans, Blackstone sold them his house and land, and went to settle elsewhere.

The land thus purchased was divided among the settlers, who, for convenience' sake, built their houses along the paths made by Blackstone's cow. Some people say that this accounts for the crooked streets in old Boston, for such was the name this settlement received soon after it was made (1630). Six acres, however, were set apart as the Common, or pasture ground, for everybody. This part of Blackstone's farm still bears that name, but it is now in the very heart of the city of Boston, a beautiful, well-kept park, and no longer a mere pasture ground.

The Boston colonists had brought tools, cattle, and seed in abundance; but in spite of all their foresight and supplies, their first winter proved very hard. It was very cold, and as they had to go some distance for their fuel, many could not secure enough. We are told that one man was even caught stealing wood from Winthrop's pile. Now, the Puritans considered stealing almost as bad as murder, and had the man been publicly accused, they would perhaps have condemned him to death. But Governor Winthrop was so good and gentle that he merely said he would cure the man of the habit of stealing, and did so by sending the rascal all the fuel he needed until spring.

Like the Plymouth colonists, the Puritans were threatened with starvation long before their ships could return. Winthrop then generously supplied the people's needs from his own store, and actually gave the last flour he had in his house to a poor man who came to beg. But the good governor did not suffer on account of his generosity, for that very day the returning ships sailed into port, bringing plenty of provisions for all.

The colony now prospered greatly, and sent home such encouraging letters that more and more people ventured across the ocean. Winthrop sent for his wife, and a minister wrote to his friends that "a sup of New England air is better than a whole draught of Old England's Ale."

During the next ten years, more than twenty thousand English-speaking persons came over to New England. There, in time, they formed fifty parishes, or villages, connected by roads and bridges. Some of these settlements were planted far inland, although the Puritans at first declared they would never need more land than what was inclosed in a circle drawn ten miles around Boston.

A governor was elected to rule over the colony, and each town ruled itself. But the people also sent representatives to the General Court, or Assembly, where public matters were discussed and laws were made for the good of the whole colony.

The government being in the hands of the people, and the Puritans wishing their children to be well educated, public schools were soon provided in every village, and in 1636 the General Court started the first college. It was located in a spot which was called Cam´bridge, in honor of the great university town in England. Two years later, a minister named Har´vard left his library of about two hundred and fifty books and some money to the new college, which since then has borne his name.

XXXIII. STORIES OF TWO MINISTERS.

At first, Harvard College had only a very few students, who were to be educated for the ministry. All the colonists contributed to the support of the institution, for those who were too poor to give twelvepence in money were told to bring a measure of corn or some fire wood. Four years after the college was founded, the first English printing press was set up there, and began to print books of psalms for the Puritan churches.

While the new college was training missionaries for the Indians, the latter had found a good friend in John El´i-ot, who came over to America in 1631. While preaching in Boston and Rox´bur-y, Eliot learned the Massachusetts Indian language, and began to translate the Bible into that tongue. It took him nearly thirty years of patient work to do this, in the midst of all his preaching and teaching. But his Bible was the first printed in

America, and many of his "praying Indians," as the converts were called, learned to read in it.

Eliot was a sweet, simple, and very lovable man. He was so generous that once, in paying him his salary, the parish treasurer tied it up in the good man's handkerchief with several knots, so that he should not be able to give it all away before reaching home. But Eliot, unable to undo these hard knots when he met a poor woman, gave her handkerchief and all, saying: "Here, my dear, take it; I believe the Lord designs it all for you."

After years of faithful work among the savages, Eliot, the "Apostle of the Indians," died, at the age of eighty-six. He tried harder than any other Puritan to convert the red men, who lost their best friend when he passed away. The Bible he worked so diligently to translate still exists; but as there are no Massachusetts Indians left, it is now of no use, except to remind us of Eliot's great patience and perseverance.

As the soil was poor, hands few, and the harvests too scanty to supply food for all, the colonists soon began to wonder how they could earn money. Before long, they discovered that by sending fish to England, they could get all the food they wanted. For that reason they fished diligently, and soon used a huge codfish as an emblem for the Massachusetts Bay colony. Next, the colonists built a large ship called the *Blessing of the Bay*, in which they sent lumber to the West Indies. In exchange for timber, they got sugar and molasses, from which they made rum to ship to England. Thus commerce was begun, and, increasing year by year, finally made the Massachusetts Puritans both rich and independent.

The Puritans, as you have seen, left England because they were not allowed to worship there as they pleased. But although they did not like it when the English tried to make them obey the Anglican Church, they now wanted to force all who came among them to think just as they did.

One young man, Roger Williams, came to New England in 1631, and preached for a while at Salem. But as he openly said that the Puritans had no right to punish people for thinking differently about religious matters, or for such trifles as smoking on the street or laughing too loud, he soon displeased some of the colonists.

They sent him away for a while, thinking he would change his mind; but when Williams came back to Salem, he insisted harder than ever that every man had a right to think just as he pleased, to worship God as his conscience bade him, and to vote whether he went to church or not. He also declared that the land around there belonged to the Indians and not to the King of England. These opinions seemed so wicked to the good Puritans that they called him up before their Council to reprove him.

Williams Welcomed by the Indians.

Finding that the Puritans would not let him live in peace in any part of the colony, but intended to send him back to England to be tried, Williams secretly escaped from Massachusetts, and went to live among the Indians. As he knew their language, and had made friends with them, he spent a very peaceful winter in their camp.

When spring came, Williams wanted to settle at See´konk; but as the Plymouth people claimed that part of the land, he went farther still, to a place which he called Prov´i-dence. Settling there, in 1636, on land he bought from the Indians, Williams was soon joined by others who shared his opinions, and thus a colony was formed in what is now Rhode Island, where all except Jews were allowed to vote. This was considered very generous in those days, although it now seems unfair to exclude anyone on account of religion.

Because Williams was so much broader-minded than many other people of his time, he has often been called the "Apostle of Toleration"—a word which means letting others alone, or allowing others to do as they please. People of every belief came to settle in Williams's neighborhood before long, and there was soon such a variety of them that it was said if a man had lost his religion he would be sure to find it again in Rhode Island.

XXXIV. WILLIAMS AND THE INDIANS.

One of the first important persons who followed Williams to Rhode Island was Mrs. Anne Hutch´in-son. Soon after her arrival in Massachusetts, in 1634, she began to hold meetings and to preach. The Puritans, who did not believe in women's talking in public, told her to be silent; but she refused to obey, and went on preaching until she gained great influence over many people.

Indeed, when an Indian war broke out, her followers even refused to go and fight unless she was allowed to talk just as much as she pleased. But as soon as the war was over, Mrs. Hutchinson was banished. Then she, too, went to Rhode Island (1637), where she bought from the Indians the large island of that name. She gave them only twenty hoes, ten coats, and forty fathoms of wampum in payment for it, and near one end of it she began the town which is now the beautiful city of New´port. Several Quakers, driven out of the Massachusetts colonies by the Puritans, also came to live near her, and her settlement prospered greatly.

Other colonies were also begun farther north. A short time after the founding of Plymouth, Mason and Gor´ges received from the king a grant of land. Coming over to America, they divided their land and founded colonies, Gorges in Maine and Mason in New Hamp´shire. Among the principal settlements thus made were the towns of Ports´mŏŭth and Dover. Some years later, however, these places were added to Massachusetts, to which colony New Hampshire was joined for about thirty-five years.

In 1630, at the time when Boston was founded, some fishermen reported that the Con-nect´i-cut River flowed between very fertile banks. This news made Lords Say, Brooke, and others ask for a grant of land there, which the king readily gave them. These owners then prepared to found a new colony, which was called Say´brook, after two of their number. But they very soon found that there was no time to lose if they wanted to claim the land the king had given them, for the Dutch had already built a trading station where Hartford now stands, and were threatening to occupy all the Connecticut valley.

In spite of the fact that the Dutch got there first, Winthrop's son was told to build a fort at the mouth of the Connecticut, or Long River, where he was soon joined by a colony of about fifty men. These settlers suffered greatly from lack of food and proper shelter.

Carrying Mrs. Hooker to Hartford.

Still, the white men spread rapidly in Connecticut, and in the spring of 1636, Pastor Hooker, "the light of the western church," came there from Massachusetts, with about one hundred men, women, and children. Walking through the woods, driving their cattle before them, and carrying poor sick Mrs. Hooker on a litter, these colonists came to settle on the banks of the Connecticut, where they founded Hartford. They brought written laws with them, in which, among other things, it was stated that a man need not be a church member to vote.

But the Connecticut colonists soon met two foes in this new region; they were the Dutch and the Pe´quot Indians, of whom the latter proved by far the more troublesome. Soon after murdering one settler, the Pequots carried his family off to Block Island. The news of murder and capture no sooner reached Massachusetts, than ninety men set out, under John Endicott, to punish the Indians.

Sailing to Block Island, the Indian stronghold, they killed the Indians and burned down their village. Then some of them went on to the Connecticut valley, to join and help the English there. The Pequots, angry with the colonists, now sought the friendship of the Narragansett and Mo-he´gan Indians; for they thought that if three such powerful tribes joined forces, the white men would soon be crushed.

When the settlers heard of this, they were terrified. But knowing Roger Williams was the only man who could prevent the Narragansetts from making an alliance with their foes, they hastily sent him a message, imploring his aid. Instead of acting meanly, as some other men would have done in his place, and leaving those who had treated him ill to look out for themselves, Roger Williams set out right away, although a terrible storm was then raging.

Narrowly escaping death, he paddled bravely on in his frail skiff till he came to the Narragansetts' camp. There he found the Pequots fiercely urging their friends to fight by showing them the bloody scalps they had already taken. During the next three days and nights, Williams pleaded and argued with the Narragansett Indians, and he finally persuaded them not to take part in the Pequot war. Thanks to his efforts, too, the Mohegans sided with the white men, their chief bravely helping John Mason, the commander of the settlers' force.

After a night spent in prayer, the combined force of colonists and friendly Indians suddenly attacked the principal Pequot camp in what is now southeastern Connecticut. Taken unawares, the savages, roused by the barking of their dogs, sprang out of their wigwams, only in time to see the white men rush into their fort. A moment later, the invaders flung blazing torches at their dwellings, which were soon in flames over the heads of their wives and children. Many perished in the fire, and the glare of the flames allowed the colonists to see and kill nearly all their dusky foes.

Soon after this massacre, the Pequot chief was overtaken and slain, and his head was long exposed on a tree, in a place since known as Sachems Head, or Point. The few remaining Pequots either became slaves or fled to the Hudson River. This was the first real Indian war in New England (1636-1638). After it was all over the colonists along the Connecticut were left in peace, and for nearly forty years there was no more trouble with the red men.

The Pequot war was scarcely finished when three hundred English settlers came to found New Haven. They were mostly rich trading people, and they wanted to have a colony which would be governed only by the laws of the Bible. The New Haven colony grew fast, and before long included Saybrook and five other very prosperous towns.

It was in the Pequot war that the colonies first saw the advantage of helping one another, and five years later (1643) a league was formed between Massachusetts Bay, Plymouth, Connecticut, and New Haven. Maine and Rhode Island were not allowed to join it, because they were not Puritan colonies. But New Hampshire really belonged to it, as that colony had been joined to Massachusetts in 1641.

XXXV. THE QUAKERS.

While the English were founding the New England colonies, many changes had taken place in England. King James I. was succeeded by Charles I., and the English, weary of monarchs who did not keep their promises, rose up in rebellion in 1643.

By this time, the English Puritans had increased so that they became masters of the whole country. It was governed by their chief, Oliver Crom´well, and called the Commonwealth of England. The Puritans, being in power, made the Roman Catholics and the Church of England people as uncomfortable as the latter had once made them. Many Catholics and Anglicans were therefore only too glad to cross the ocean, in their turn, so as to found new homes where they could worship as they pleased; and you shall soon hear how they prospered.

Cromwell, as Protector of the Commonwealth of England, made a new law (1651), called the Navigation Act. By this law it was decided that the colonists should build no more ships, and that all their goods should be carried across the ocean only in English vessels. This law was very unjust, and captains of English ships speedily took advantage of it to raise their prices for freight. So, while England was rapidly growing rich, her colonists grumbled sorely at the heavy rates they had to pay.

That same year began the great Quaker excitement in Massachusetts. The Quakers were the disciples of a very good man, George Fox. They called themselves Friends, but were called Quakers by the other people, because they often said one ought to quake at the thought of the wrath of God.

As some of the months and days of the week bore the names of old heathen gods, the Friends would not use them, but, instead, numbered the days and months, speaking of the first day of the sixth month, the twelfth day of the second month, and so on. They would not take any oaths, either, but used only the words "yea" and "nay." They further treated all persons alike, calling even the king by his given name, and refused to take off their hats in his presence. Although generally quiet and modest, a few of the Quakers were so anxious to spread the teachings of their preacher Fox that they came over to Massachusetts, knowing they would be illtreated there.

Nevertheless, they began preaching, and firmly but quietly refused to stop when told to do so. They were therefore tortured and punished in many ways. A few were whipped, sent to jail, or put in the stocks. Their books were burned; they were driven out of the colony; and as all this was not enough, four of them were hanged.

The Quaker excitement finally grew so great that some of them were sent back to England and the rest forced to take refuge in Rhode Island, where they could practice any religion they liked. But the Quakers who had been shipped back to England, and especially a few discontented colonists, complained very much of the Massachusetts government, and made considerable trouble for New England.

XXXVI. THE KING-KILLERS.

Cromwell having died in 1658, the English, most of whom were still greatly attached to the royal family, soon begged Charles II. to come back and take possession of his throne. He gladly returned to England, where he punished no one for the revolution, except the men who had condemned his father, Charles I., to death. A few of these king-killers, or "reg´i-cides," as they were called, fled from England as soon as they heard the king was coming, and three took passage for America.

Two of these men, Goffe and Whal´ley, after some trouble, reached the New Haven colony, where Puritan friends helped them to hide. The king sent orders to arrest them, and magistrates began to search every house to secure the regicides. For about eighteen years these two men lived in constant dread of being caught; but, thanks to their many friends, they always escaped. They dwelt for a while in a deserted mill, then in a cave, and once hid under a bridge while their pursuers galloped over it, expecting soon to overtake them.

The fact that the New Haven people had sheltered some of his father's judges, added to the complaints of the Quakers and discontented colonists, displeased Charles II. greatly; and he finally declared that New Haven should cease to form a separate colony, and joined it to Connecticut, which received a new charter (1662).

It is also said, however, that these two colonies were united mainly to please the Connecticut people, because they had won the king's favor by sending him a pretty message to welcome him back to the throne. The charter he gave them was the most liberal ever granted the colonists, although the one Roger Williams secured for Rhode Island also granted many privileges.

You doubtless remember the treaty made between the Indian King Massasoit and Governor Carver, when the Pilgrims first came to Plymouth. This treaty was kept forty years, and Massasoit and his tribe faithfully helped the colonists to fight the other Indians. But when Massasoit died, his two sons, who had received the names of Alexander and Philip, began to rule in their turn.

Alexander knew, by the wampum belts which were the history books of his tribe, that nearly all the land of his Indian fathers had been sold to the white men, piece by piece. It had been given in exchange for beads, kettles, blankets, etc., and now very little was left. But the Indians fancied that, although they had sold the land, they could still hunt and fish there as much as they pleased. The colonists, however, would not allow them to do so, and drove the Indians farther and farther off, until they began to feel cramped for space.

It is said that when one of the colonists once came to bid an Indian chief to remove still farther from the white settlements, the red man invited him to take a seat beside him on a log. Crowding nearer and nearer his guest, the chief bade him move again and again, until he forced him to the very end of the log. But when the colonist declared he could not move another inch without falling off, the chief calmly answered: "It is just so with us. We have moved as far as we can go, and now you come here to ask us to move farther still."

This feeling of unfair treatment made Alexander so angry, at last, that he formed a secret alliance with the Narragansett Indians to kill all the white men. But the Plymouth governor, hearing of this, promptly sent for him, bidding him come and clear himself of the accusation of treachery. Then, as the Indian did not obey at once, Winslow quickly set out, with his men, to bring him by force.

Alexander, furious at being thus compelled to mind, fell seriously ill from fever. The colonists then allowed his followers to carry him home; but on the way back, the Indian chief breathed his last. Ever after, his people were in the habit of saying that he had gone to the Happy Hunting Grounds, where the palefaces could never come to crowd him out.

XXXVII. KING PHILIP'S WAR.

At Alexander's death, Philip became chief of his tribe; and thinking the English had poisoned Alexander, he began to plot revenge. After brooding over his wrongs for several years, Philip was accused of planning to attack the colonists. The governor of Plymouth sent word to Philip to come and explain his conduct, but, we are told, the Indian haughtily said to the messenger: "Your governor is but a subject of King Charles of England. I shall not treat with a subject. I shall only treat with the king, my brother. When he comes, I am ready."

An Indian Attack.

Still, Philip did come, and promised to keep the peace. But a few years later, he was about to fall upon the colonists unexpectedly, when a praying Indian warned them of their danger. This Indian was murdered by three of Philip's friends, who were found guilty and put to death for the crime. Not long after this, the Indians attacked the colonists at Swan´sea, as they were walking home from church, and killed all those who could not escape in time to the blockhouse.

As had been agreed beforehand, an alarm was sent right away to Plymouth and Boston, where signal fires were kindled on what is still known as Beacon Hill. An army of colonists hastily obeyed this summons, and set out to attack Philip. But the latter was too quick for them, and managed to escape from his camp at Mount Hope, with about seven hundred Indians.

Small villages and outlying farmhouses were now in constant danger; for the savages, gliding along as noiselessly as snakes, pounced upon the people by day or by night. They forced their way into the houses, killed and scalped the men, carried women and children off into captivity, and left nothing but heaps of smoking ruins behind them.

In the course of this terrible war, several women were carried off with all their children. One child—a tiny babe—annoyed one of the savages by crying, so he killed it in the poor mother's arms. The unhappy woman, too ill to walk as fast as the Indians wished, was also slain; but the rest of her children were sold into captivity. In time, all were rescued, except one little girl, who later married an Indian, and never saw her family again until she was a grandmother.

In the course of King Philip's War, which lasted from 1675 till 1678, forty out of ninety English towns suffered greatly, and thirteen were burned to the ground. Although there were no great battles,—except a swamp fight, in which about one thousand Indians were killed,—there were many small engagements, one of the fiercest being that of Bloody Brook, near Deerfield. It seems that, owing to an alarm, the village was deserted, but nearly one hundred men were sent there to save the crops. On their way back, they carelessly laid their guns in a cart, and scattered to eat grapes. The Indians, lurking in the forest in great numbers, took advantage of this to fall upon them unawares, and seizing their weapons, killed all but a few of them.

The Indians treated all their captives cruelly, and often made them suffer horrible tortures. Terrible stories are told of this time, when many died, and but few captives escaped. Once, the savages suddenly broke into a house, and a servant hastily thrust a little child under a big kettle to hide it from them. The little one kept so very quiet that the Indians did not know it was there, and later on it was found unharmed. We are also told that a woman once drove a party of Indians away by flinging ladlefuls of boiling soap at them, which made them flee, shrieking with pain. Another band of Indians, creeping into a house by way of the chimney, were killed on the hearth, one after another, by a mother who thus bravely defended her little ones.

Once, while the people of Hadley were at church, some Indians came sneaking into the village; but they were seen by the king-killer Goffe, who happened to be hiding just then in the minister's house. Rushing out, that white-haired old man gave the alarm, and led the colonists so boldly that the Indians were driven away. But as soon as the danger was over, Goffe again disappeared, and was never seen in public again, although he is said to have died at Hadley a few years later, and to have been buried in the minister's cellar.

All these secret attacks and massacres roused the anger of the colonists, who finally got the better of their savage foes. Philip's wife and son fell into their hands, and we are told that when the Indian chief heard that his child had been sent to the West Indies, to be sold as a slave, he bitterly cried: "My heart breaks! I am ready to die."

Shortly after, the camp where he and his tribe were rapidly starving to death was surrounded by Captain Church's little army. Philip fled, hoping yet to escape; but a bullet from an Indian's gun struck him, and "he fell upon his face in the mud and water, with his gun under him." When his body was found thus, his head was cut off, and set up on a pole in Plymouth, where it was kept for about twenty years. To reward Church for his services to the colony, the settlers gave him Philip's wampum belt, which has always been carefully kept as a great curiosity; and the sword which he handled in King Philip's War can still be seen in the rooms of the Massachusetts Historical Society.

XXXVIII. THE BEGINNING OF NEW YORK.

Charles II. was such a very merry and easy-going king that whenever his followers asked him for land in America, he readily granted it to them. In fact, he was so free-handed that sometimes he even gave away what really did not belong to him! Thus, he told his brother James, Duke of York, that he could have all the country claimed by the Dutch, saying that it was English because Cabot had visited it first.

As you will see, this led to trouble; for the Dutch, after building their first trading post on Manhattan Island, in 1614, had begun to form a colony in the New World. At first, the Dutch settlers were on very good terms with the Indians; but, owing mostly to the fire water they so freely sold, quarrels soon arose.

Seeing this, the Dutchman Min´u-it purchased the whole of Manhattan Island, in 1626, for about twenty-four dollars' worth of beads and trinkets. The town on it was called New Amsterdam, after a great city in Holland, and this sale, which gave the Dutch land for one sixth of a cent an acre, was soon followed by many others. Indeed, they soon owned all the Hudson and Delaware valleys, besides a strip of coast between the mouths of these two rivers.

Under Governor Kieft, the Indians, exasperated by the treatment they received, planned to murder all the Dutch. But a grateful Indian gave a colonist timely warning of the coming danger. Kieft now tried to make friends with the redskins, and appointed a meeting with their chiefs on Long Island. When called upon to state their causes of complaint, the Indians brought forth a bundle of sticks, and laying them down, one after another, related a special wrong for each stick.

Realizing that they had good cause for complaint, Kieft made a treaty with them, which, however, was soon broken. Again farms were attacked and settlers were scalped, and it was only after the number of whites had been greatly reduced, and more than a thousand Indians killed, that peace was finally made, in 1645. It was during this war that Mrs. Hutchinson, who had left Rhode Island and settled in the western part of Connecticut, was slain, with all her children except one, who was carried off into captivity.

To induce people to come and settle in the New Netherlands,—as the Dutch called their share of the New World,—rich settlers, or patroons, were promised a farm of sixteen miles' water front, provided they brought out fifty colonists with the necessary farming tools and stock. The result of this offer was that many comfortable Dutch houses arose in the New Netherlands, which soon had many prosperous settlements, in each of which was a free school, so the children should not grow up ignorant.

These colonists were simple-hearted, jolly, and fond of good things to eat. On their numerous holidays they danced gayly, a pastime which the Puritans considered very wicked, and they often assembled to help one another and have a good time. Their principal festivals were held in honor of St. Nicholas, and on January 1, when they called upon all their friends to wish them a happy New Year.

In 1656, about ten years after the Indian troubles ended, there were about one thousand inhabitants in the city of New Amsterdam, which stood on the lower part of Manhattan Island. Protected on three sides by the waters of the North and East rivers and the Bay, the town was cut off from the rest of the island by a high palisade running from shore to shore. This was called the "Wall," and the place where it once stood is still known as Wall Street. Beyond this palisade were many farms, among others one on Bowery Lane, which belonged to Peter Stuy͘´ves-ant, the fourth governor of the city.

The settlers having been driven away from Fort Nassau, on the Delaware, by the Indians, some Dutch merchants soon sent Swedes to form a colony on the spot where Wil´ming-ton now stands. The country around there was therefore called New Sweden. But the newcomers could not live in peace with the Dutch; so Governor Stuyvesant attacked them, seventeen years later, and took possession of their town, so that New Sweden ceased to exist.

Stuyvesant wanted the People to resist.

It was while this fighting governor was at the head of affairs that King Charles's brother James, admiral of the English navy, first claimed his new territory. His ships appeared unexpectedly at New Amsterdam, and the astonished Stuyvesant soon received a letter ordering him to surrender the city. Although Stuyvesant had but one leg, he was a brave man, and wanted the people to resist. But they refused to fight, and made him so angry by their talk of yielding that he tore the English letter all to pieces.

In spite of his rage, however, New Amsterdam surrendered, and Stuyvesant had to march out of the town and return to Holland. The Dutch flag was hauled down and replaced by the English; but, as the city had been seized in time of peace, Holland soon showed her displeasure by declaring war against England. Vessels were sent out to retake New Amsterdam, which surrendered the second time as easily as the first, and the Dutch again ruled over their city.

But when the war was all over, the whole province of the New Netherlands was given up to the English. New Amsterdam's name was changed to New York (1664), and Holland never again claimed any part of our country. But the Dutch settlers continued to occupy their farms, and there are many people now in America who proudly claim descent from the early settlers of the New Netherlands. Interesting stories are told about the Dutch settlers, the most famous of all being Washington Irving's tales of Sleepy Hollow and of Rip Van Winkle.

The Duke of York, owner of all the land in the New World which had once belonged to Holland, shortly gave part of it to two of his friends, who called their tracts East and West New Jersey. The owner of West New Jersey did not keep his share long, but sold it to some Quakers, who settled near Bur'ling-ton. East New Jersey was likewise sold to William Penn and others; but both provinces were given up to the crown in 1702. New Jersey—as they were now called—was under the same rule as New York—until 1738, when it became a separate colony.

XXXIX. PENN AND THE INDIANS.

In the meantime, the Friends in England had greatly increased in number. There were now many rich and clever people among them besides William Penn, who was a scholar and a preacher. He had become a Quaker in spite of all his father's efforts to make him a courtier, for the elder Penn was an admiral, and a great friend of Charles II., to whom he lent large sums of money. As the king could not repay this money, William Penn suggested, after his father's death, that Charles should give him, instead of all other payment, a large tract of land in the New World.

Charles was only too happy to clear his debt in such an easy way. He therefore made Penn a grant of woodland, which he insisted upon calling Penn-syl-va'ni-a ("Penn's Woodland"). But we are told that Penn tried to bribe the clerk to write the name "Sylvania" only, as he thought it absurd that the land should bear his name. In exchange for this tract, all the king asked was two beaver skins a year, and one fifth of all the gold and silver found there. The land secured, Penn prepared to carry out a long-cherished plan, which was to found colonies of Friends in the New World. For that purpose, he had already bought a share in the West New Jersey colony, and, in 1682, he crossed over to America himself.

As soon as Penn set foot in West New Jersey, we are told that the colonists brought him a sod in which was planted a green twig, to show that he owned the land and all that grew upon it. Next they presented him with a dish full of water, because he was master of the seas and rivers, and with the keys of the fort, to indicate that he was in command of the army and had all the power. Penn graciously accepted these offerings, and, as you shall see, made a noble use of his authority over his province. Although Pennsylvania had been given him by the king, he rightly considered the Indians the real owners of the soil, and decided to pay them for it.

Benjamin West, Artist.

Penn's Treaty.

He therefore sent for the chiefs, whom he met under a huge elm. Penn came among the Indians unarmed, and, after smoking a peace pipe with them, bargained for the purchase of a large tract of land. Under this elm he also made a treaty which lasted for more than sixty years,—"the only one never sworn to and never broken."

On this occasion Penn made a speech, to which the Indians replied by saying: "We will live in peace with Penn and his children as long as the moon and the sun shall endure." Then the two parties exchanged gifts, the Indians bestowing upon the Quaker a wampum belt on which a paleface and a redskin were represented hand in hand. This belt is still carefully kept by the Pennsylvania Historical Society.

The elm under whose branches this interview took place was carefully preserved for many years. Even during the Revolutionary War, sentinels mounted guard over it, so that none of its branches should be cut off for fire wood. But in 1810 it was unfortunately blown down, and a monument, bearing the inscription, "Unbroken faith," now marks the spot where Penn and the Indians first met.

Before crossing the Atlantic, Penn had written out laws for his province, granting his people the right to do as their conscience bade in religious matters, to vote, and to be tried by a jury of twelve men. He now added that if there was any trouble between an Indian and a settler, the case was to be tried by six Indians and six colonists, to make sure that justice should be equally well meted out to both parties.

When the Quakers first left England for the New World, people made great fun of them, declaring that, since the fighting Puritans, Dutch, and Virginians had such hard times with the Indians, the Quakers, whose religion forbade them to return blow for blow, would soon be killed. They were greatly mistaken, however, for none of the colonies suffered less from the natives than Pennsylvania.

The Friends were so gentle that they treated every one kindly, and a little story will show you how good and generous even the children were. We are told that a little girl sat at the door of a log house, one day, eating her milk porridge. Her mother heard her softly say again and again: "Now, thee sha'n't;" then, "Keep to thy part." As no one was near, the mother stole up on tiptoe to find out to whom the child could be talking. Imagine her surprise when she saw her little girl sharing her supper with a big black snake, which ate from one side of the bowl while she helped herself from the other, patting him on the head with her spoon whenever he tried to come over to her side!

It was Penn himself who founded the first town in his grant. He called it Phil-a-del′phi-a, or the "City of Brotherly Love," because he wished all the people to live in peace together, like one family. The first houses were built of wood; then brick dwellings were seen; and each cottage was soon surrounded by a neat garden, in which bloomed gay flowers. Many Germans came over before long, at Penn's invitation, and settled just north of Philadelphia, in what is still known as Ger′man-town.

These were joined by other colonists, from different parts of central Europe; and as the English did not perceive any difference between the various forms of the German language and that used in Holland, they generally called all the newcomers Dutch. These settlers managed to understand one another, however, by using a strange dialect, which is still heard in some parts of Pennsylvania, where it is now known as "Pennsylvania Dutch."

As Pennsylvania had no seacoast of its own, Penn was glad to buy some land south of him,—called Del′a-ware, in honor of one of the governors of Virginia. Having placed his colony on a good footing, Penn went back to England. He had spent much money in doing this, and was no longer as rich as he had once been. Besides, his opinions got him into trouble, and we are told he went to prison rather than pay what he thought an unjust debt. For a time he was even deprived of his lands; but they were finally given back to him, and he and his heirs ruled Pennsylvania until the Revolution.

Old Swedish Church at Wilmington, Delaware.

It was within the limits of Delaware that the Dutch, as we have seen, had built Fort Nassau. They were driven away by the Indians, and that part of the country belonged for seventeen years to the Swedes, who called it New Sweden. At the end of that time, however, it again fell into the hands of the Dutch, who, about eighteen years later, finally gave it up to the English, with all the rest of the New Netherlands.

Thus within less than fifty years Delaware had completely changed hands four times, when it was purchased by Penn as seaboard for his state. For a time it was part of Pennsylvania; but after 1703 it had an assembly of its own, and it is counted as one of the thirteen famous English colonies founded in North America.

XL. THE CATHOLICS IN MARYLAND.

When Henry VIII. made a change in the national church, many Catholics became discontented, and longed to leave England and settle elsewhere. Later, Lord Bal´ti-more decided to make a home for Catholics in the New World. As Newfoundland, where he tried to plant his first colony, proved too cold, he came to Virginia, in 1629. But the Virginians, being Church of England people, refused to receive any Catholics in their midst.

Thus driven away from Virginia, Lord Baltimore crossed to the opposite side of the Po-tō´mac. He asked for a grant of land here, which was given, in 1634, to his son. He promised to pay the king two Indian arrows every year, with one fifth of all the gold and silver he found. This tract was called Ma´ry-land, in honor of the Catholic Queen Henrietta Maria, and prosperous settlements were made at St. Marys and at An-nap´o-lis. Unlike their Protestant neighbors, these Catholic colonists would not allow any one to be persecuted for religion, and as all except Jews could vote, people of every faith soon came thither, and Maryland was rapidly settled.

This colony, however, had its troubles, too. There was first a quarrel with Virginia, and then several Indian wars; and when William became King of England, he took the government away from its Catholic proprietor. But later on, Baltimore's heirs, having turned Protestant, recovered their rights, and were left in control of the whole province until the time of the Revolution. Maryland's chief city, Baltimore, was founded about 1729. It was named in honor of the Catholic founder of the colony, and it still contains thousands of faithful Roman Catholics.

Owing to mistakes made in drawing up the different grants, the boundary between Pennsylvania and Maryland became a cause for disputes which lasted about fifty years. Several times surveyors were sent out from England to settle the quarrel, and the line they finally drew is generally known as the Mason and Dixon line. At the end of every mile, these surveyors set up a stone post, bearing on either side the initial of the colony it faced; and every five miles, a larger pillar, with the arms of both families, the Penns and the Baltimores.

While all the changes we have been describing were thus taking place in the rest of the New World, Virginia had not been standing still. Indeed, it had prospered so greatly that it had become the most important of all the colonies. But its progress was interrupted several times. For instance, three years after the founding of the House of Burgesses, a quarrel between an Indian and a settler ended in a murder, which brought about an Indian war.

Powhatan, who had vowed that the sky should fall before the Indians broke peace with the Virginians, was now dead. The savages, hating to see their former hunting and fishing grounds occupied by the planters, now attacked the scattered settlements, and murdered men, women, and children. Even Jamestown itself would have been surprised, and all the colonists slain, had not a friendly Indian given the people timely warning.

Terrified by this Indian outbreak, the colonists no longer dared occupy their plantations, and either crowded into a few of the towns or went back to England. In a short time the colony thus found itself reduced by half, although the Indians were beaten in the war. Some years later, seeing that the Indians were rising again, and that nothing but severe measures could save the settlement, another war was begun, and all the hostile Indians were either driven away or slain.

When King James I. heard that the colony was failing, he fancied that the trouble arose from poor laws and bad government; so he took away the Virginia charter, and made the colony a royal province, in 1624. But although he boasted that he would soon make new and better laws for Virginia, he never did so. His son and successor, Charles, after whom one of the capes at the entrance of Chesapeake Bay had been named by the first settlers, also found too much to do at home to trouble himself about the Virginians, who were sorely tried by tyrannical governors.

Still, although they lived on the other side of the Atlantic Ocean, the colonists loudly insisted that they had the rights of free-born Englishmen. They therefore said that the governors the king sent over could not tax them or make new laws, except through the House of Burgesses. But as the governors would not always agree to this, quarrels arose, which gradually became more and more bitter.

XLI. THE OLD DOMINION.

It was while Governor Berke´ley ruled Virginia that Puritan England revolted against and beheaded King Charles I.; and soon after that they made Cromwell Protector of the new republic, or Commonwealth, of England. When these tidings came to Virginia, many of the colonists were indignant. Just as in England, the people sided for or against the king, the Puritans being called "Roundheads," while the Royalists claimed the title of "Cav-a-liers´."

The latter were by far the more numerous in Virginia, and as they prided themselves upon their great loyalty, they invited Charles II., son of the beheaded king, to come over and rule their colony, which they now affectionately called "the Old Dominion." Charles did not accept this invitation, and Parliament, deciding that the colony should obey England, sent out a new governor. The latter, upon arriving in Virginia, declared that, according to the new Navigation Act, Virginia, like all the rest of the colonies, would have to send its produce to England in English ships.

This law was very unjust, and the English captains who came into the bays and up the rivers for cargoes, now charged higher rates to carry produce to England. They could not get good prices for it in England, had to pay high prices for the goods they bought there, and, besides, asked heavy freight rates for bringing these goods back to the planters in Virginia. The colonists thus got little in exchange for their tobacco and other produce. They were also greatly annoyed, for even the goods they wished to send to the neighboring colonies, or to the West Indies, had to be carried first to England and then back again, unless they paid a heavy duty.

This was unfair, and the Virginians did not like it. Still, it did not prevent their colony from increasing rapidly, for many of the Royalists, finding life unbearable under Puritan government in England, came out to America. Here they talked a great deal of the royal family, prided themselves upon being true to the exiled king, and when the news finally came that Cromwell was dead (1658), many Virginia planters openly rejoiced.

Two years later, the royal family was restored in England, and the House of Burgesses recalled Governor Berkeley, who had ruled there in the days of Charles I. But the Burgesses warned him that, while they were loyal subjects of the king, they were fully determined to make their own laws, and that his duty would consist mainly in seeing that these were duly obeyed.

Although the colonists thought their troubles would end when the king had come to the throne, they soon found out that Charles II. was a worse master than Cromwell. Always in need of money, the king not only kept up the hated Navigation Act, but, as Virginia had become the property of the crown in 1624, he now made a present of it to two of his friends, Lords Cul'pep-per and Ar'lington (1673), telling them they might keep it for thirty-one years, and have all the money they could make from it.

These two noblemen, hearing that there were about forty thousand people in the Old Dominion, fancied they would be able to tax them as much as they pleased; but the colonists, who were proud of their rights and homes, grumbled at this change of owners, and said they would obey no one except the king.

Jamestown was then the only city in Virginia; but each plantation formed a small colony by itself, and people traveling from place to place were always hospitably entertained in the houses they passed. The estates were so large and scattered that there were very few schools; but the richest colonists hired private tutors for their children, and sent their sons to the English universities to complete their education. In this, Virginia was different from the Northern colonies, and the greater part of her people were ignorant. Thinking they would therefore be easier to rule, a Virginia governor once boasted of the fact that they had neither printing press nor free schools, and added that he hoped they would not have any for the next hundred years!

XLII. BACON'S REBELLION.

IN the midst of the trouble caused in Virginia by the change of owners, and the increased taxes they imposed, the Indians, who had been quiet for about thirty years, suddenly came back. They said that while they had sold the land to the English, they still had the right to fish and hunt wherever they pleased. A dispute about this question again resulted in a murder, which—for history often repeats itself—occasioned another war.

Since Berkeley took no steps to defend them from the savages, who boldly attacked outlying plantations, the Virginians determined to act themselves, and chose Nathaniel Bacon as their leader. But Berkeley declared they were rebels, and hearing that they had started, he would have pursued them, could he have raised troops.

Bacon's Rebellion.

When the Virginian army came home in triumph from the first brush with the Indians, Bacon was called before the governor and tried as a rebel. But the jury promptly acquitted him, to Berkeley's great disgust. The governor waited until war broke out again, and when Bacon was too busy fighting to offer any resistance, he declared him an outlaw. This accusation, added to grievances about the taxes, caused a short civil war in Virginia, during which Jamestown was seized by the rebels, and Berkeley fled.

But the governor returned as soon as Bacon was called away, and prepared to defend himself in Jamestown. Hearing of this, Bacon came back, ready to lay siege to the city. The angry governor ordered out the cannon to shoot the rebels; but we are told that Bacon, having captured the wives of Berkeley's men, now put these women in front of his little force, knowing their presence there would prevent any bloodshed.

Ruins of Jamestown.

Thus routed by a "white-apron brigade," Berkeley fled a second time; and Bacon, fearing he might return and fortify the city, burned Jamestown to the ground (1676). The first English city built in the United States thus became a heap of ruins, and no trace of it now remains, except a small part of the old church tower and a few gravestones.

Shortly after the burning of Jamestown, Bacon fell ill and died, his followers sadly crying: "Who is there now to plead our cause?" Their helpless grief was so great that Berkeley took advantage of it to return. He then began to punish all those who had taken any part in what is known in history as "Bacon's Rebellion," or the "Great Rebellion" in Virginia.

In fact, Berkeley showed himself so cruel that many of those who had borne arms were condemned to die. Once, when a prisoner whom he particularly hated was brought before him, he angrily cried: "You are very welcome; I am more glad to see you than any man in Virginia; you shall be hanged in half an hour." This prisoner was executed, and so many others shared his fate that King Charles, hearing how Berkeley abused his power, indignantly cried: "The old fool has taken away more lives in that naked country than I for the murder of my father."

XLIII. A JOURNEY INLAND.

When Berkeley was called back to England in disgrace, none of the Virginians were sorry to see him leave. But the new governor sent out by the owners was no better, for he laid such heavy taxes upon the people that the king finally had to take back the gift he had made to his friends. Virginia, therefore, once more became a royal province. But shortly after, King Charles died, and his Catholic brother, James, had to put down a rebellion in England before he could occupy the throne in peace. James was very resentful; so many of those who had taken up arms against him were sentenced by a harsh English judge to be shipped to Virginia and sold there as slaves for a term of ten years.

But although both king and judge had decreed that none of these poor prisoners should be allowed to buy their freedom, the Virginians generously set them at liberty as soon as they landed. The governor, seeing it would make trouble if he tried to oppose the Virginians in this, made no great objection, and after that no white men were ever sold as slaves in America.

Before long, too, another improvement was made; for the Virginians, feeling that it was necessary to have a college of their own, sent a messenger to England for a charter. Although the king's ministers swore at this man at first, and told him that Virginians ought to think of nothing but tobacco, permission was finally granted, on condition that two copies of Latin verse should be sent to England every year. The college thus founded—the second in our country—was called William and Mary, in honor of the king and queen who succeeded James II. in 1688.

Some years later, Governor Spots'wood built himself a beautiful house in Virginia, which he ornamented with large mirrors. But the woods were still so thick there that we are told a deer strayed into the parlor one day. Catching a glimpse of his reflection in a tall mirror, he rushed up to the glass and dashed it to pieces with his horns!

This same Spotswood was of an adventurous turn of mind, and wishing to see what lay beyond the Blue Ridge Mountains, he once set out on a journey of exploration. It is said that he and his jolly companions crossed both the Blue Ridge and the Al'le-gha-nies, coming home after a ride of about one thousand miles, delighted with the beautiful country they had found on the other side of the mountains.

They sent such a glowing account of this journey to King George I. that he knighted Spotswood, giving him a coat of arms bearing a golden horseshoe. Some writers add that, in memory of this long ride, Spotswood founded an order of knighthood in Virginia, which included all those who had made part of the expedition, and their direct descendants.

XLIV. THE CAROLINA PIRATES.

You remember, do you not, how Raleigh tried and failed to plant a colony on Roanoke Island, in what is now North Carolina? For about seventy-five years after this, that part of the country was left to the Indians and the few settlers who strayed there from Virginia. But in 1663 Charles II. gave a large tract of land to several of his favorites, who were called the lords proprietors. To flatter the king, they named the country Carolina, the very name which the French had given it many years before, in honor of their monarch, Charles IX.

Now, the lords proprietors wanted to make this colony different from all the rest by placing all the power in the hands of the rich and noble, as was arranged by a code of laws drawn up by John Locke. But these laws could never be used, and to induce people to settle in Carolina at all, the lords proprietors had to promise them large tracts of land, freedom of thought, and a share in making the laws.

This granted, Quakers, Huguenots, Puritans, Scotch, Irish, English, Swiss, Germans, and Dutch came there in great numbers. In the north, the colonists devoted themselves to lumbering, tobacco-raising, and the production of tar, pitch, and turpentine; but in the south, they grew a great deal of rice, indigo, and tobacco, and many sweet potatoes.

At first, the French Huguenots tried to raise silkworms in their new colony; but they soon had to give up this attempt, because the climate proved too damp. Still, although unfavorable for silkworms, Carolina proved just right for the growing of rice. The first seed was brought to the governor of Charles'ton by a Mad-a-gas'car ship captain, who bade him plant it in marshy soil. There the rice grew so well that before long all the swamps were turned into rice fields, and Carolina rice is now famous in all parts of the country.

Some fifty years later, a planter's daughter tried to raise indigo. After several failures, she succeeded in doing so, and indigo was raised in Carolina until the time came when cotton paid better. Thanks to its rice, tobacco, indigo, and marine supplies, Carolina became so rich and prosperous that, although it was the twelfth English colony, it soon outstripped several of the rest. The Carolina planters, growing rich, bought many negroes to work their large tracts of land, and spent the greater part of the year at Charleston, where they led a gay life and entertained a great deal.

Carolina was also noted for her bold seamen, for all along the coast there were many small harbors, in which pirates could hide. They sailed out of these places to attack vessels on their way to and from the West Indies, and often secured much booty. The best known of all the Carolina pirates was Blackbeard. Like Captain Kidd of New England, he is supposed to have buried great treasures in the sand along the coast, and there are still people foolish enough to try to find them.

The Spaniards, who still held Florida, had always been jealous of the English. When the latter came to settle in Carolina and Georgia, the Spaniards, hoping to drive them away, stirred up the Indians to war against them, and sometimes took part in the fights themselves. Besides, many disputes arose about the boundaries, both parties being equally inclined to claim all the land they could.

In 1729 the lords proprietors ceased to have any control over their lands, which, divided into North and South Carolina, became two royal provinces. These prospered much during the following years, and by the time the Revolutionary War began, North Carolina ranked fourth in importance among the colonies.

We have now seen how twelve of the English colonies were planted on our coast, and before traveling northward once more, to see how New England was getting along, you shall hear how the thirteenth and last colony was founded, in 1733.

James O´gle-thorpe, a kind-hearted Englishman, perceiving the suffering of debtors, who were then imprisoned like criminals, longed to give them a chance to begin life over again. Thinking they could best do this in the New World, he asked George II. for a tract of land there, promising to hold it in trust for the poor. This territory was called Georgia, in honor of the king; and Oglethorpe, having assembled his colonists, sailed for America.

Arriving at Charleston, he went southward and founded the city of Sa-van´nah. Before doing so, however, he had an interview with the Indians of that section, from whom he bought the land. In exchange for his gifts, they presented him with a buffalo robe lined with eagle feathers, saying: "The eagle signifies swiftness, and the buffalo strength. The English are swift as a bird to fly over the vast seas, and as strong as a beast before their enemies. The eagle's feathers are soft, and signify love; the buffalo's skin is warm, and means protection: therefore, love and protect our families."

An attempt to cultivate olive trees and breed silkworms proved as great a failure in Georgia as in Carolina; but rice soon became one of the staples of the colony, and the first fine cotton was raised there from seed brought from India. Oglethorpe, wishing to give his colony a good start, said that neither rum nor slaves should be allowed within its limits. But some of his colonists were displeased at this, although both Oglethorpe and John Wesley—the founder of the Methodist Church—tried to convince them that they would be far better off if they did their own work and kept sober. Shortly after the visit of the Wesley brothers, White´field also came out to visit the Georgia colony, where he supported the first orphan asylum built in our country.

In 1739, war having broken out between England and Spain, Oglethorpe led a small army of Georgians into Florida, to besiege St. Augustine. To punish the Georgians for this attempt to take their city, the Spaniards invaded their land three years later, but only to be defeated at the battle of Fred-er-i´ca. When these troubles came to an end, Oglethorpe went back to England. But even before his departure people began to change the laws, and in a few years they introduced both rum and slavery. Although Oglethorpe gave up Georgia to the king in 1752, he took a great interest in the settlement he had founded, and as he lived to be very old, he saw it join the other colonies in 1776, for it was one of the famous thirteen.

XLV. CHARTER OAK.

After King Philip's War was over in New England, Charles II. turned his attention to the colony of Massachusetts Bay, where four things did not suit him. The Navigation Law, which applied to all the colonies, was not kept in Massachusetts; there were many quarrels between that colony and the settlements in Maine; Massachusetts would not have an Episcopal church; and it had coined money. To punish the colony for these things, Charles took away its charter (1679), and said that thereafter New Hampshire should form a separate royal province.

The Massachusetts people were, of course, angry at being deprived of their charter; still, they managed to keep the money they had minted. These coins bore on one side a rudely stamped pine tree. Charles having asked to see one of them, the man who showed it to him carefully explained that the picture represented the Royal Oak, whose branches had concealed the king when Cromwell's soldiers were seeking for him. This clever explanation so amused the merry monarch that he allowed Massachusetts to retain its "pine-tree shillings." We are also told that the mint master was allowed a certain number of these coins as pay. When his daughter married, he made her sit down in one scale, filled the other with "pine-tree shillings" till the scales balanced, and gave her with this dowry to his new son-in-law, telling him he now had a wife who was really worth her weight in silver.

When James II. came to the throne, he sent Governor An'dros to rule over New England and New York. This man, wishing to make sure all the power would be in his hands, tried to get hold of the charters of the colonies. But when he asked the people of Rhode Island to give up theirs, they gravely answered they did not have any.

The Charter Oak.

Next, he went to Hartford and asked the Connecticut Assembly to surrender their charter. The people, unwilling to give it up, argued about the matter until it grew so dark that candles had to be brought into the room. Seeing that the governor would yet compel them to obey his orders, a patriot, Captain Wadsworth, suddenly flung his cloak over the candles, and taking advantage of the darkness and confusion, seized the charter, which he cleverly hid in a hollow oak. This tree stood in Hartford until 1856, when it blew down; but the spot where the Charter Oak once stood is now marked by a monument.

As there were no matches in those days, it took time to relight the candles; but as soon as that was done, Andros again demanded the charter. No trace of it could now be found. Andros, in a rage, then called for the record books of the colony, and writing *Finis* ("The End") at the bottom of the page, declared he would rule Connecticut without any charter at all.

He next proceeded to Boston, where he made the people equally angry by insisting upon holding Episcopal services in the Old South Church, by laying extra taxes upon them to pay for the building of a fine new chapel, and by trying to assume all the power. His tyrannical ways finally made the Bostonians so indignant that they put him in prison.

Some of the governor's friends, who were called Tories, because they sided with the king, now tried to rescue him. They cleverly smuggled women's garments into the prison, and Governor Andros, dressed like a lady, would have gotten out of prison safely had not his big feet roused the suspicions of the guard. Shortly after, he was sent to England to be tried, and although he later governed Virginia, he never came back to New England. His master, James II., being as much disliked in England as Andros was in the colonies, had

68

meanwhile been driven out of the country, where his son-in-law and daughter, William and Mary, came to reign in his stead (1688).

The New England people, like most of the English, were delighted with this change of masters. They had cause to be, for Connecticut and Rhode Island were now allowed to keep their old charters, while Massachusetts received a new one, by which the Plymouth colony and Maine were added to it, and by which the right to vote and partly govern themselves was assured to the people.

But we are told that Governor Fletcher, who ruled over Connecticut after Andros, had so little respect for its charter that he once went to Hartford to assume command over the militia there. He, too, was met by Captain Wadsworth, who, having called out his men as requested, bade them beat the drums every time the governor tried to have his orders read.

This scene must have been very funny; for while the governor roared, "Silence!" Wadsworth loudly cried, "Drum! drum, I say!" Finally the captain laid his hand on his sword, saying very firmly: "If I am interrupted again, I will make the sun shine through you in a minute." Frightened by this threat, Governor Fletcher returned in haste to New York, and never made another attempt to tamper with the Connecticut charter.

At about the same time an interesting meeting was held by several Connecticut ministers at New Haven. They had decided they needed a new school, so each man brought a few books, which he laid down on the table, saying they were his contribution to the new institution. This school was held in different places at first, but in 1718 it took the name of Yale College, because a man of that name gave some books and money for its use.

A few of the old Tories, both in England and America, remained faithful to the banished James, and among them was the governor of New York. When William and Mary were proclaimed rulers, this governor fled, leaving the colony without any head. Leīs´ler, a patriotic citizen, knowing the French and Indians in the north would take advantage of this state of affairs to invade the province, now rallied his friends around him, and with their help began to govern for William and Mary.

But as Albany at first refused to obey Leisler, there was some trouble and bloodshed. Soon a messenger came over from England, to say that the king and queen were going to send over a new governor, named Sloughter. This messenger bade Leisler, in the meantime, give up the power to him; but the patriot refused to do so, and surrendered it only to Sloughter when he finally came.

Because of this refusal, Leisler and eight of his friends were accused of treason, and sentenced to death. But Sloughter, feeling that the trial had been hardly fair, would not sign their death warrants, so they could not be put to death. Leisler's foes, therefore, had to wait until a dinner party took place, when they made the drunken governor sign the papers, and hanged Leisler. A few years later, the whole affair was brought before Parliament, which declared that Leisler had died innocent, and paid his family a certain sum of money because he had been wrongfully accused and killed.

XLVI. SALEM WITCHES.

About four years after the Revolution of 1688, in England, arose the Salem witchcraft delusion, which you will now hear about. In olden times, as you have seen, people had very few and poor chances of learning, compared with what you have now. Almost everybody then believed in witches. These were supposed to be persons who had sold their souls to Satan, could ride through the air on broomsticks, make others ill by looking at them with an evil eye, cast a spell upon cattle, houses, or furniture, and, in short, do all sorts of impossible things.

As you know, some children have very lively imaginations, and hearing people talk of such things as seriously as if they were quite true, a few children in Salem, Massachusetts, began to fancy they must be bewitched, because they were not quite well and had fits. The grown-up people, who should have known better and merely given the children medicine to cure their illness, believed these youngsters, and anxiously inquired who could have cast a spell upon them.

The children, remembering that their elders often spoke of the witches as old, first began to talk of such and such a woman who had looked at them crossly or threatened to beat them with her staff when they played tricks upon her. These poor old creatures, who were really in their second childhood, and not responsible for what they said or did, were put into prison, and tortured in many cruel ways, so as to force them to confess that they were witches. Bewildered, and hoping to get free, some of the poor old creatures finally acknowledged that they were witches.

Almost everybody believed in witchcraft at that time, and for many years supposed witches had been treated with great cruelty in Europe. When persons accused of witchcraft refused to confess, some people thought that the only way to find out the truth was to throw them into the water. If the victims sank, it was said they could not be witches, but if they swam, it was considered a sure sign that they had sold themselves to the Evil One, and they were sentenced to death, either by hanging, burning, or torture. But this was, after all, only a choice of deaths, for the poor creatures who sank were allowed to remain under water so long, to make sure they were innocent, that they were generally dead when taken out.

Persons who were only suspected of witchcraft were put in the stocks, fastened to the pillory, whipped at the cart tail, or placed on the ducking stool, or had their ears chopped off. These were punishments often applied to criminals in those days, and if you care to see pictures of pillory, stocks, and ducking stool, you can find them in any large dictionary. Both men and women were accused of witchcraft in Salem, and one of the men was put to death by a torture called *peine forte et dure*, by which he was slowly crushed under a thick door, upon which tremendous weights were laid. He was, fortunately, the only person in our country who was ever punished in this inhuman way.

Nearly one hundred and fifty people of all kinds were arrested for witchcraft in Salem, and nineteen of them, after being tried by a court, were found guilty and put to death. But people finally saw that it was all folly, and even the learned minister, Cotton Math´er, who had believed in witches just like the rest, had to own that he had been mistaken. The children were now punished when they pretended to be under a spell, and the Salem witchcraft delusion came to an end. Ever since then, no one with a grain of sense has believed in witches; but you will often hear people speak of the terrible time they had in Salem while the belief in them lasted. The building shown in the picture was one of the houses of Salem at that time; and it is still pointed out there as "the witch house."

The Salem Witch House.

Mather, the famous "Patriarch of New England," who believed in witches, was a very learned man. He wrote more books than there are days in the year, and was so busy that he wrote over his door, "Be short," so that people should not take up his time with idle talk. In one of his books he once read that smallpox could be prevented by vaccination. He told this to Boylston, a Boston doctor, who tried it on his own son and servants. But when the Bos-to´ni-ans first heard of it, they were so indignant that they wanted to kill Boylston.

In time, however, people saw that the doctor was right, and ever since vaccination has been practiced, few people have died of the disease which once swept away whole families. Because Boylston went ahead and did what was right, in spite of people's threats, he is now greatly honored, and a fine street in Boston bears his name.

XLVII. DOWN THE MISSISSIPPI.

While the English were planting thirteen colonies along the Atlantic seaboard, between Nova Scotia and Florida, the French were equally busy farther north. As we have seen, Breton fishermen visited the banks of Newfoundland early in the sixteenth century, and gave their name to Cape Breton Island. Verrazano and Cartier both crossed the Atlantic in behalf of the French, Cartier naming the St. Lawrence, Canada, and Montreal, and claiming all Acadia (the land east of Maine), together with New France, which was situated in the basin of the Lakes and the St. Lawrence River.

Religious troubles had, as we have also seen, led Coligny to try to plant colonies in Carolina and Florida. But the Huguenot settlers were murdered by the Spaniards, and the attempt of De Monts (mawN) to establish a colony in Maine proved equally unsuccessful. The first real settlement of the French was made at Port Royal (Annapolis), in Acadia (Nova Scotia), in 1604. This colony, composed of thrifty people, in time became prosperous, and the Acadians lived in peace and comfort in their new homes, being on excellent terms with all the neighboring Indians.

In 1608, Champlain (sham-plān´), the "Father of New France," a noble, brave, and good Frenchman, crossed the Atlantic for the fourth time. He sailed far up the St. Lawrence, and made a settlement at Quebec, which soon became the chief French town in America. Champlain explored the country for hundreds of miles around there. He was the first European to behold the lake which bears his name, the same year that Hudson sailed up the river to Albany (1609). During these explorations of New France, Champlain made friends with the Al-gon´quin Indians, the great foes of the Ir-o-quois´ (or Five Nations), who occupied all the central part of what is now New York state.

Old Quebec.

The Algonquin Indians, being at war with the Iroquois, persuaded Champlain to help them. His presence in armor in the next battle, and the report of European firearms, so terrified the Iroquois that they were badly beaten on the shore of Lake Champlain. This ever after made them hate the French as cordially as they did their lifelong enemies, the Algonquin Indians. To be able to cope with the latter, who easily got firearms from French traders, the Iroquois began to buy guns from the Dutch; for their usual weapons, tomahawk and bow and arrows, were far less effective than firearms.

The French had come to Quebec with two great purposes in view: the first, to trade for furs, and the second, to convert the Indians. The colonists were, therefore, either trappers, traders, or missionaries. The former went about from place to place to set their traps or trade with the Indians, and were therefore called *voyageurs* (travelers), or *coureurs de bois* (wood rangers). Finding the European dress unsuited to the rough life they led, these men soon adopted a half-Indian costume of soft deerskin, and learned many of the woodland ways of the redskins.

Wherever the trappers and traders went, priests boldly followed, carrying only a crucifix, a prayer book, and sometimes a portable altar. They diligently taught, preached, and baptized, making every effort to learn the Indian languages as quickly as possible, so they could preach the gospel and win more converts. Full of zeal for their religion, these missionaries were so brave that they soon won the respect of the Indians; and when the latter saw how quietly the priests endured hardships of all kinds, they lent an attentive ear to their teachings.

Both traders and priests were on very friendly terms with the Indians, whose good will they retained by living among them and by making them frequent small presents. As the French hunters considered the Indians their equals, they soon married squaws, and their children, being half Indian and half French, strengthened the bonds between the two races.

Little by little, priests and traders pressed farther and farther inland, visiting the Great Lakes, along whose shores they established missions, forts, and trading posts. Finally, they came to what are now Il-li-nois' and Wis-con'sin, where many places still bear the French names then given them.

The most remarkable of all these French traders was Joliet (zho-le-ā'). Not only was he thoroughly at home in the trackless forests, but he could also talk several Indian languages. Hearing the savages tell of a great river flowing southward, he fancied that it must empty into the Pacific Ocean.

Joliet had long been the companion of Marquette (mar-ket'), a Catholic priest, so they two resolved to go and explore that region. But the Indians tried to frighten them by telling them there were awful monsters on the "Father of Waters," which swallowed men and canoes.

Fron'te-nac, the governor of New France, having consented to this journey, Marquette and Joliet met at the outlet of Lake Mich'i-gan (map, page 322), paddled up to Green Bay, and went up the Fox River. Then their Indian guides carried their canoes across to the Wisconsin River, where, bidding them farewell, the trader, priest, and five voyageurs drifted down the stream to the Mississippi. This was in 1673. Sailing southward for many miles, without seeing a single human being, the explorers came to huge cliffs upon which the Indians had painted rude demons; then they beheld wide prairies and great herds of buffaloes on the right bank of the river.

Some distance farther on they saw a path, and, following it, they came to an Indian village. When the Indians saw the white men draw near, the chief came out to welcome them, shading his eyes with his hand, and saying: "Frenchmen, how bright the sun shines when you come to visit us!" To honor his guests, he had a feast of buffalo meat and fish prepared, and fed the strangers with a huge wooden spoon, just as if they were babies. Other Indians removed fish bones for them with their fingers, blew on their food to cool it, and from time to time poked choice bits into their mouths. As these were Indian good manners, Marquette and Joliet submitted as gracefully as they could. But it seems that it hurt their host's feelings when they refused to taste his best dish, a fat dog nicely roasted!

Marquette and Joliet come to an Indian Village.

After spending the night with these Indians, Joliet and Marquette were escorted back to their canoes. Paddling on, they next came to the place where the Missouri joins the Mississippi. The waters of the Missouri were both swift and muddy, and whirled whole

72

trees along as easily as mere chips. After passing the mouth of the Ohio, the explorers saw Indians armed with guns and hatchets, which proved they were near European settlements.

Fully convinced by this time that the Mississippi flowed into the Gulf of Mexico, and not into the Pacific Ocean, as they had first supposed, and anxious to make this fact known at Quebec, the explorers turned back, south of the mouth of the Arkansas (ar′kan-saw). They had thus reached nearly the same place which De Soto had visited about one hundred and thirty-two years before. Slowly paddling upstream, they now worked their way up the Illinois River, and carried their canoes overland to the Chicago (she-caw′go) River, through which they reëntered Lake Michigan, after eighteen months' journey.

Marquette staid at a mission on Green Bay for a while, then journeyed to the Illinois, and when spring came again, he made an effort to get back to Mich-i-li-mack′i-nac. But he became so ill that before long he had to be carried ashore, and laid under a tree, where he breathed his last, and was buried.

Meantime, Joliet hastened back to Montreal to make his report to the governor. His canoe upset, and his plans and papers were lost, but the news he brought made the French anxious to secure the land by building trading forts along the rivers that had been explored.

It is because Marquette and Joliet were the first white men who visited this part of the country, that their names have been given to a port and county at the northern end of Lake Michigan, and to a town in Illinois. They were such bold explorers that beautiful monuments have also been erected in their honor.

XLVIII. LA SALLE'S ADVENTURES.

In the meantime, another French explorer, La Salle (lah sahl′), had also been at work, and had discovered the Ohio River. In 1679, six years after Marquette and Joliet sailed down the Mississippi, La Salle came to the Illinois River, where he built Fort Crèvecœur (crāv′ker) ("heartbreak"), near the place occupied by the present city of Pe-o′ri-a.

La Salle next went back to Canada for supplies, and reached Montreal only by means of much paddling and a long tramp of a thousand miles. But he left orders with a priest, named Hen′ne-pin, to explore the upper part of the Mississippi River. Father Hennepin, therefore, went down the Illinois, and then paddled upstream to the Falls of St. An′tho-ny, in 1680. His adventures were very exciting, for he fell into the hands of the Sioux (soo) Indians. Long after he got back to Europe, he claimed to have been the first to sail all the way down the Mississippi; but this honor is now generally believed to belong to La Salle.

When La Salle came back to Crèvecœur a year later, he found his fort in ruins; most of his men had deserted. At first he thought that his few faithful followers had been killed by the Indians, but his fears were quieted when they joined him at Michilimackinac.

In 1681 La Salle again set out, with his lieutenant Ton′ty and a band of Indians, for the southern end of Lake Michigan. Sailing up the Chicago, he had his canoes carried across to the Illinois River. It was the Indians who taught the white men thus to pass from one stream to another, and to avoid falls and rapids. These carrying places received from the French explorers the name of "portage," by which they are still known, even though no one now thinks of using them for that purpose.

Sailing down the Illinois and Mississippi, La Salle reached the mouth of the latter stream in 1682. As was the custom with explorers of every nation, he solemnly took possession, in the name of his king, of the river and the land it drained. This territory, as you can see on your map, included most of the region between the Rocky and Alleghany Mountains, the Great Lakes, and the Gulf of Mexico; it was called Lou-i-si-a′na, in honor of Louis XIV. of France.

Arriving at Quebec, after meeting with many adventures, La Salle told Frontenac that France ought to make good her claim to the land by building trading posts at intervals all along the principal streams. He added that it was also necessary to have a fort at the mouth of the Mississippi, and soon after went to France to tell the king about his discoveries, and ask for help.

Louis XIV. gave La Salle several ships loaded with supplies; and a small army of colonists having joined him, the explorer set out. His fleet reached the Gulf of Mexico in 1684; but, owing to some mistake, it sailed past the mouth of the Mississippi without seeing it. As the captain would not believe La Salle and turn back, they coasted on until they finally landed at Mat-a-gor′da Bay, in Texas.

Here a fort was built; but the spot proved so unhealthful that many colonists died. The ships having gone back, run aground, or been dashed to pieces, the French could not get away again by sea. La Salle therefore decided to set out on foot, so as to join Tonty and obtain more supplies for his unhappy colony.

As had been agreed, Tonty had come down the Mississippi to meet La Salle. But after waiting vainly for him several months, he went northward again, leaving a letter in the fork of a tree, and telling the Indians to give it to the first white man they saw. Long before reaching this place, La Salle's men became angry because their expedition had been a failure. They blamed their leader for all their sufferings, and, falling upon him unawares, basely murdered the man who is known as the "father of French colonization in the Mississippi valley."

Although La Salle was dead, his plan was too good to be abandoned. Some thirteen years later, therefore, a Frenchman named Iberville (e-ber-veel′) came out from France to found a fort at the mouth of the Mississippi. He sailed up the stream, and received from the Indians Tonty's letter, which, they gravely said, was a "speaking bark." As Iberville found no good place for a fort near the mouth of the "Father of Waters," he built Bil-ox′i, on the coast of what is now the state of Mississippi.

Shortly after, a party of Frenchmen, exploring the banks of the river, saw an English ship sailing upstream. The newcomers said they had come to build a fort on the Mississippi; but the Frenchmen either deceived them by telling them this was not the stream they sought, or gave them to understand they had come too late. So the English turned around and sailed away, and ever since that bend in the great river has been called the "English Turn."

Iberville's brother, Bienville (be-aN-veel′), in 1718 built a fort and established a colony on the spot where New Or′le-ans now stands. He gave the place that name in honor of the French city of Orleans.

There was no more trouble with the English, but this colony came very near being swept away by the Natch′ez Indians, who made an agreement with the Choc′taws to fall upon the white men on a certain day and hour, and kill them all. To make sure that there should be no misunderstanding, each chief was given a small bundle of sticks, with directions to burn one every day, making the attack only after the last had been consumed.

An Indian boy, seeing his father burn one of these sticks, stole two, and secretly set fire to them; and though he thus found out that they were nothing but ordinary wood, his theft made his father attack the French two days too soon.

Instead of a general raid upon all the settlements, only one was surprised, two hundred men being killed, and the women and children carried off into captivity. The other French colonists had time to arm, and they defended themselves so bravely that the plans of the Indians came to naught.

XLIX. INDIANS ON THE WARPATH.

The French were in possession of Acadia, New France, and Louisiana. The immense tract of land drained by the St. Lawrence and Mississippi rivers was rich in fur-bearing animals, whose pelts were brought by Indians and trappers to the missions and trading posts. There they were loaded in canoes and floated down the Lakes and the St. Lawrence, or down the Mississippi, so as to be shipped to France from Quebec and New Orleans.

You might think that the French would have been satisfied with all they had, but they were not. They longed to control the Hudson also, which they claimed for France, because they said Verrazano had first visited New York Bay. Besides, Champlain had come within a few miles of where Albany now stands, shortly before Hudson sailed up the river bearing his name.

Longing for an excuse to drive the English away from the Hudson valley, the French were glad when war was declared, in 1689. Their king sent over Count Frontenac to be governor of Canada again, and to lead in the struggle with the English. Frontenac was a good general, and had much influence over the Indians. He is said to have joined in their war dances and athletic sports, in spite of his old age, and to have boasted of the tortures he meant to inflict on his English foes and their Iroquois allies.

But when Frontenac arrived in Canada (1689), he found that the Iroquois had struck first. They had destroyed some French villages, had killed many settlers, and had even roasted and eaten some of their captives in sight of Montreal. On the other hand, some Indian allies of the French had surprised Dover, in New Hampshire. Here dwelt Major Wal′dron, who had taken part in King Philip's war. To avenge the capture of two hundred of their race at that time, the savages now tortured Waldron to death, cutting off his hand to see how much it weighed. To their amazement, the scales marked just one pound! This awed them greatly, for although the traders had always told them that a white man's hand exactly balanced a pound of beaver skins, they had always doubted the truth of that statement. Half the people in Dover were killed, the rest carried off into captivity, and the town reduced to ashes.

The next winter (1690), Frontenac sent a small band of French and Indians against the village of Sche-nec′ta-dy, New York, on snowshoes. They arrived there in the dead of night. The place was defended by a high palisade, but the inhabitants felt so sure no one would attack them that cold night, that they had left both gates wide open, and guarded only by huge snow sentinels set up there in fun.

Roused from sound slumbers by blood-curdling Indian war whoops, a few escaped, but only to die of cold on their way to Albany. Many of the rest were killed by the attacking party, who, after burning the place to the ground, withdrew with their captives and plunder.

In the course of this struggle,—which is known in our history as "King William's War," because it took place during that monarch's reign,—the French and Indians attacked many villages in New York and New England. The most daring of all their attempts was against Hā′ver-hill, a town not very far from Boston. Here much property was destroyed, and many people killed or captured.

There are countless stories told of the deeds of valor done by men, women, and even little children in those terrible times. You shall hear the story of Hannah Dustin, of Haverhill, as an example. This poor woman was just recovering from illness, and was alone in the house, with her baby and nurse. Seven other children were out in the fields with their father, who was busy with his plow. All at once, they were startled by a war whoop. Mr. Dustin, seeing the Indians between him and his house, and knowing he could not save his wife, bade the children run to the blockhouse, while he bravely covered their retreat.

Mr. Dustin defending his Children.

Father and children reached the fort in safety; but the Indians rushed into the house, killed the baby by dashing its head against the wall, and carried both women off as captives. After several days' march and much ill treatment Mrs. Dustin, her nurse, and two captive boys made up their minds to escape. One of the boys had learned from an Indian how to kill and scalp a foe; so one night, when their captors were asleep, the four prisoners noiselessly rose, seized tomahawks, and killed and scalped ten Indians. Then they took a canoe, and with some trouble made their way home. Mrs. Dustin received fifty pounds reward for those scalps, besides a present from the governor of Maryland, who admired her pluck. That people might not forget what hard times the settlers had, her statue has been placed in Concord, New Hampshire, where you can see her grasping a tomahawk, ready to kill her foes.

As long as the war lasted, New Englanders and New Yorkers defended themselves as bravely as they could. But Indian foes were very hard to fight, because they always fell upon people unawares. In their anger, the colonists finally determined to carry the war into the enemy's country. They therefore sent out a fleet under Sir William Phips, to attack and destroy Port Royal, in Acadia. This being done, the fleet tried to take Quebec, while armies from New York and Connecticut attacked Montreal. But both these attempts failed, and when the war was ended by the treaty of Rys′wick (1697), neither party had gained anything, although many lives had been lost.

L. TWO WARS WITH THE FRENCH.

Both the French and the English suffered greatly during King William's War, but the peace which followed it did not last long. Five years later, "Queen Anne's War" brought about new sufferings, and more deeds of heroism.

We are told that, urged by a French priest, the Indians built a church at St. Re′gis, in Canada. Wishing to have a bell to hang in the tower of this chapel, each convert brought a pelt, and the bell was ordered from France. But on its way over, it fell, by accident, into the hands of the English, who hung it up in the town of Deerfield, in Massachusetts.

The Indians, feeling that the bell belonged to them, and egged on by their priest, made a sudden raid upon Deerfield, in 1704, and, after killing or capturing many of the people, rescued their bell from the English meetinghouse, or church, and carried it off to St. Regis. They were so delighted with it that it is said they rang it every step of the way. This bell was cracked over a hundred years later, and the Indians, who still prized it greatly, carried it to Troy, where they had it refounded, while they mounted guard over it day and night.

France and Spain were allies in this war, so the trouble was not confined to New York and New England. The Spaniards made a raid from St. Augustine, and vainly attacked Charleston. A few years later, the New Englanders conquered Acadia, and at the treaty of U'trecht, in 1713, the British received this province, Newfoundland, and the land around Hudson Bay. But Acadia's name was now changed to Nova Scotia, and Port Royal was called Annapolis, in honor of the English queen.

For the next thirty years peace reigned unbroken; still, during that time the French began to build their chain of sixty forts along the Lakes, the Ohio, and the Mississippi, thus drawing a line from the mouth of the St. Lawrence to the mouth of the Mississippi. Most of these forts have since become cities, and you will find that many of them still bear the French names given by their founders. Their strongest fort, however, was at Lou'is-burg, on Cape Breton Island. It was so well fortified that the French boasted that even women could defend it against a large army.

NORTH AMERICA
BEFORE THE FRENCH AND INDIAN WAR

The third struggle with the French and Indians, which began in 1744, is known in our country as "King George's War," and in Europe as the "War of the Austrian Succession."

Now, Louisburg was so near Annapolis that the colonists felt sure the French would set out from there to recover Acadia. They therefore sent a messenger to England to explain their danger and beg for troops to protect them. But the prime minister knew so little about America that the messenger had to show him Louisburg and Annapolis on a map. He was so surprised then to discover that Cape Breton is an island, that he ran off to tell it to the king as a great piece of news.

Seeing that the British did not supply much help in answer to their appeal, the colonists before long made up their minds to take Louisburg themselves; and an army of them bravely set out from New England, under the leadership of Pep'per-ell, in 1745. After six weeks' siege, and many deeds of daring, these four thousand New Englanders took the fortress, and when the news reached Boston the people almost went mad with joy. Three years later, however, this joy was turned to equally deep sorrow, for when the treaty of Aix-la-Cha-pelle' (1748) was signed, the fortress was given back to France, in exchange for the town of Ma-dras' in India.

Three wars had now been fought between the French and the English, but the vexed question as to who should own North America was not yet settled. The French had, as you have seen, taken possession of the Mississippi valley; but although some rumors of their presence there had reached the colonies, very few people really knew what the country was like, and what a vast tract of land France could thus claim.

Many of the English colonies had received grants of land running "from sea to sea," and now that population was increasing rapidly, people began to talk of crossing the Alleghany Mountains to settle on the other side. They were eager to do so, because hunters brought back to Virginia glowing descriptions of the Ohio, or "Beautiful River," the "Gateway of the West," and of the fertile lands through which it flowed. Just at this time, the governor of Virginia heard that the French were on the point of building a fort on the Allegheny River, so he bade George Washington, a young surveyor, find out if this news was true, and carry a letter to the French officer there to warn him that the Ohio country belonged to Virginia.

LI. WASHINGTON'S BOYHOOD.

As you are going to hear a great deal about Washington, it will interest you to learn something of his family and his youth. Two Washington brothers came over from England to Virginia about the year 1657, and settled near the Potomac River. Augustine Washington, the grandson of one of these men, married twice, and had, in all, ten children. His eldest son by his second wife was born on February 22, 1732, and named George. Shortly after his birth, the family went to live on the Rap-pa-han´nock River, and there George spent his early childhood. He was a fearless, strong, hot-tempered little lad, but, having good parents, was even then taught to control his passions.

As he is the greatest man in our history, many stories, true and untrue, are told about him. Perhaps the most famous is about his new hatchet. We are told that Father Washington planted young cherry trees in his garden. He visited them daily to see how they throve, and was very angry when he saw, one day, that a favorite tree was badly hacked. On all Virginia plantations, there were many negro children always running about. Thinking one of these had done the mischief, Augustine Washington was about to punish him, when his little son stopped him, saying: "Father, I cannot tell a lie; I did it with my little hatchet."

Washington was sent to a small school near by, and his blank books, which can still be seen, show what a careful, painstaking student he was. In one of these books he copied a set of rules for good behavior, which he even then tried to put into practice, and of which the last two were: "Let your recreations be manful, not sinful," and "Labor to keep alive in your breast that little spark of celestial fire called conscience."

When Washington was only twelve, his father died, leaving an estate to each of his sons. The care of the six younger children and of their property was left to his wife, a good and very sensible woman. She was very strict, and brought up her children so carefully that they all filled well their places in life. Indeed, her eldest son, George, like most truly great men, often said that he owed his mother more than words could ever tell.

Washington was always fond of all athletic exercises, and as a lad delighted in riding the wildest horses on the plantation. Among these was one young colt of such a fiery temper that no one was allowed to mount him. One day, the temptation to do so became too strong for George, and he suddenly sprang upon the horse's back. The colt tried to throw him off, and, failing to do so, dashed off at such a rate that he burst a blood vessel and fell down dead.

Washington and the Colt.

Washington, dismayed at the result of his disobedience, went silently home. At table, his mother asked her guests if they had seen her beautiful young horse. Covered with blushes,—for he was always modest and reserved,—Washington now confessed what he had done. Although Mrs. Washington keenly regretted the death of the colt, she showed no anger, but quietly said: "It is well; but while I regret the loss of my favorite, I rejoice in my son, who always speaks the truth."

She was so fond of this son that when one of his half-brothers wanted him to serve in the British navy, she refused to let him go. As soon as Washington had finished school, he went to live with this brother at Mount Vernon, where he learned to know all the people around there, and, among others, Lord Fair'fax.

This nobleman owned great tracts of land in the valleys of the Alleghany Mountains, and as they had never been surveyed, he hired young George to do the work. This was a very hard task, and the seventeen-year-old Washington was often, for days at a time, far away from any settlement, forced to depend upon hunting for food, and obliged to sleep out in the open air.

The Virginia Natural Bridge.

These hardships, however, only made him strong and self-reliant, and when he came back to his home, from time to time, he doubly enjoyed the amusements of the young people, and danced gayly, a pastime of which he was always fond. It was probably during one of these surveying expeditions that Washington first visited the Natural Bridge in Virginia. Here he showed his athletic skill by tossing a coin on top of it when standing almost directly under it.

We are also told that he scaled the rocks, which were then free from any except nature's marks, and reaching a high point, carved his name in the stone. For years, Washington's name is said to have stood there on the rocks, as far above all the rest as is his worth compared with that of other men. But a young man once climbed up there to carve his name above Washington's, an act of presumption for which every one scorns him. He went up so far that he could not come down again, but had to climb higher and higher, and at last be drawn to the top with a rope.

LII. WASHINGTON'S JOURNEY.

By the time Washington was nineteen, he had shown himself so capable, honest, and thoroughly trustworthy that every one who knew him greatly respected him. His brother Lawrence having fallen ill of consumption, Washington went with him to Bar'ba-dos, where he had an attack of smallpox.

This journey, the only one Washington ever made outside the limits of our country, was so interesting to him that he kept a diary in which he made note of all he saw and heard. After a winter spent in the West Indies, Washington came home to get his sister-in-law; but before they could sail to join the invalid, they heard he was coming home to die.

Washington tenderly nursed this older brother to the end, and was made the guardian of his delicate little girl. Lawrence Washington said that if his daughter died unmarried, the estate of Mount Vernon was to belong to George. In spite of all Washington's tender interest in this little niece, and of the utmost care, she did not live long, and, as his brother had wished, Washington became owner of Mount Vernon. There he began his favorite occupation as a planter, and showed himself to be as careful and painstaking a farmer as he was a surveyor.

We are told he packed his tobacco himself, and sent such good flour to the West Indies that barrels marked "George Washington" were always allowed to pass the customhouse without being examined. Besides filling his place as surveyor and planter, Washington also became major in the Virginia militia, and took great interest in all military affairs.

When the news of the Frenchmen's purpose to build forts along the Allegheny and the Ohio reached Governor Din-wid'die, he resolved, as we have seen, to send out a trustworthy person to see if it was true, and to carry a letter to the commander of the

French force (1753). His choice promptly fell upon Washington, who, receiving his instructions, and perceiving the need of haste, started out that same day to carry out the governor's orders.

He made his way across country to Logstown, where he heard that the French commanding officer was on an upper branch of the Allegheny River. He therefore went thither, and delivered his letter. But the Frenchman shrugged his shoulders, and said he would send the letter on to Governor Duquesne (doo-kān´), whose orders he was in the meantime bound to carry out. Tramping thus through the wilderness in the dead of winter, Washington found out all Governor Dinwiddie wished. Seeing he must hasten, if the French were to be checked, the young officer left his guides, baggage, and horses, and, alone with Gist,—an experienced hunter and trapper,—went back to Virginia by a short cut. During this journey he and Gist had several narrow escapes.

Once an Indian—who had probably been bribed by the French to kill them—shot at them. Gist and Washington, suspecting treachery, pretended it was only an accident; but when the Indian left them at night, promising to come back in the morning, they promptly broke camp. Pressing forward all night, they reached the Allegheny early in the morning, and found it only partly frozen. As they could not cross on the ice, as they had hoped, they plied their one dull hatchet with such a will that they soon cut down several trees and built a rude raft.

But when they got out into the stream, Washington's pole caught in the ice and jerked him out into ten feet of ice-cold water. Grasping the raft, Washington escaped; but his clothes were dripping wet, and a few moments later they were frozen stiff. The raft was now driven on an island, where Gist lighted a fire as quickly as possible; and here Washington spent the night, turning around and around so as to dry his clothes. Luckily, on the next day the travelers found that the ice was strong enough to bear them, and, crossing over to the other side of the river, they hurried on.

After visiting an Indian queen, with whom he made friends by giving her a few trinkets, Washington went on to Virginia, where he gave Governor Dinwiddie all the necessary information. The governor was so pleased with what Washington had done, and thought his news so important, that he published Washington's journal. Then, to carry out the orders he had received from England, and make sure the land south of the Ohio should not be snatched away from him, Dinwiddie raised a force of two hundred men, and sent them to build a fort at the forks of the Ohio. While these men were busy erecting their stockade, the French, one thousand strong, came down from Ve-nan´go, on the Allegheny, and, driving the English away, completed the fort for their own use, calling it Duquesne, after their governor.

LIII. WASHINGTON'S FIRST BATTLE.

When the Virginians learned that the French had driven their men away from the forks of the Ohio, and had taken possession of the fort they had just begun, they were naturally very angry. Seeing that they would lose all claim to the land unless they drove the French away, they now determined to raise enough men and money to equip an army. Before long, therefore, Washington was sent out with about three hundred men, and he was busy erecting a small breastwork (called Fort Necessity) at Great Meadows, when he heard that the French were near there.

Setting out immediately, he surprised and defeated this force; but learning that more troops were coming, he prudently retreated to Fort Necessity, at Great Meadows, which he once described as "a charming field for an encounter." Here the French and Indians soon attacked him in such numbers that, in spite of his valor, he was forced to surrender, on July 4, 1754. Washington's men had behaved so bravely that the French allowed them to march out with the honors of war; that is, taking their flag and their arms with them.

In describing this battle, Washington is reported to have said: "I heard the bullets whistle, and believe me, there is something charming in the sound." But later on, when he had seen what a sad thing war really is, and some one asked if he had ever said this, he quietly answered: "If I said so, it was when I was young!"

When Washington and his troops came back to Virginia after the battle at Great Meadows, the colonies saw that the French were fully determined to leave them no land west of the Alleghanies. They had felt so sure of this that a few weeks before the battle they sent men to Albany to discuss how they could best resist their enemies, and keep what they claimed as their own.

Still, in one sense, neither French nor English had any right to this land, for as a bewildered Indian chief remarked when he first heard of the dispute: "If the French claim all the land north of the river, and the English all the land south of it, where is the land of the Indians?"

LIV. STORIES OF FRANKLIN.

One man was to have a great share in the last French and Indian war, although he was no soldier. This man was Franklin, and as he is one of the greatest men in our history, it will surely interest you to hear a little about him.

Born in a poor family in Boston, the lad was named Benjamin, probably because he was his father's twelfth child. With so many brothers and sisters older than himself, Benjamin was not spoiled. As they were all very poor, he was often obliged, small as he was, to help his father make soap and dip tallow candles, a work he greatly disliked. But as there had been free schools in New England from the very beginning, Benjamin learned to read out of the New England Primer when only a tiny boy. He has told us many stories of himself; among others, one of his childhood which you ought to know, because it has given rise to an American proverb.

It seems that Benjamin once had a few pennies. This was a great fortune for so small a lad, and although his brothers and sisters teased him to know what he was going to buy with them, he would not tell. On the street, one day, he saw a big boy blowing a whistle with all his might. This whistle so fascinated little Benjamin that, after talking to its owner awhile, he gave all his pennies in exchange for the toy.

Marching home, Benjamin proudly exhibited his treasure, thinking he had made a great bargain and bought the finest thing in the world. His disappointment was very keen, therefore, when his brothers told him that it was only a common whistle, such as he could have bought anywhere for one penny! Ever since then, when any one pays too much for pleasure, or anything else, people have said: "He has paid dear, very dear, for his whistle."

As was the custom in all Puritan families, the Franklins had long prayers, and they said such a lengthy grace before meals that hungry little Benjamin often grew impatient. As their breakfasts generally consisted of smoked and dried herring, he once suggested that his father should say grace over the whole barrel, so that he need not stop to repeat it every time the fish was served!

81

Franklin's father was too poor to let him go on with his studies, so at twelve Franklin became apprentice to an older brother, the printer of the fourth newspaper issued in our country. Here Franklin learned to set type and to handle the rude press then in use. He also began to write, and as he did not want his brother to know it, he disguised his handwriting, and slipped his contributions under the shop door at night.

These articles, written by a boy of fourteen, proved so able that the brother read them aloud to his friends, who greatly praised them, little suspecting that they were written by the apprentice setting type in the corner. But Benjamin's elder brother proved so unkind to him that the boy left Boston at seventeen, and, embarking upon a coasting vessel, went to New York, where he vainly sought employment.

There he heard that work was to be had in Philadelphia, then the largest city in our country. A stage ran between that place and New York twice a week, making the journey in two days. This rate of travel seemed so very rapid then that this coach was generally called the "Flying Machine." But as Franklin did not have the means to pay for a seat in this conveyance, he embarked on a sloop, working his way. After several days' tacking, a long, weary tramp, and a row on the Delaware, he landed in Philadelphia early one morning.

By this time he had only a few pennies left, which, as he felt hungry, he soon gave to a baker for three large rolls. The small amount of luggage he had with him was thrust into his coat pockets, and with a roll under either arm, and one in his hand, Franklin strolled down the street, munching his bread as he walked along. A girl standing on her father's doorstep laughed at the awkward lad passing by, little thinking that a few years later she would be his wife.

Franklin's Entry into Philadelphia.

Finding employment in Philadelphia, Franklin worked hard, studying as much as he could after hours. Every book he could buy or borrow was eagerly read, and he paid small sums to booksellers for the loan of their volumes overnight, sitting up late and rising early so as to get all he could out of them. Franklin loved books so dearly that he soon learned a great deal about foreign countries. He longed to visit them, and therefore gladly welcomed a proposal to go to England and buy a printing press.

As the governor of Pennsylvania promised to supply the necessary funds, Franklin set out; but upon landing in England he found that the governor had deceived him, and that there was no money to be had. Alone in a foreign land, without means or friends, Franklin again sought employment, and worked for an English printer during the next few years. By dint of hard work and great economy, he managed to save money enough to bring him back to Philadelphia, at the age of twenty. Then, after working as clerk and printer for a while, Franklin set up in business for himself, and married.

Besides printing a newspaper,—for which he wrote the articles, set the type, handled the press, and even carted the paper to his shop in a wheelbarrow,—Franklin soon began to publish a pamphlet called "Poor Richard's Almanac." It contained not only the usual information about sunrise and sunset, the moon, tide, and weather, but many short sayings, full of good advice. They were so easily remembered, and so often quoted, that some of them have become household sayings. A few are: "No gains without pains." "Never leave that till to-morrow which you can do to-day." "Time is money." "Keep conscience clear, then never fear."

A Page from Poor Richard's Almanac.

You might think that Franklin was busy enough with all this work; still, he managed to learn a great deal besides French, German, Spanish, and Italian, which he studied alone and at night. He founded the first public
library in Philadelphia, the University of Pennsylvania, and the first fire brigade, the first insurance company, and the first hospital in the city. Besides that, he invented the first good stove, advised paving the streets, and was constantly in political office from the time he was thirty until he died, at the age of eighty-four.

Franklin was so interested in sciences that he studied them closely, too; and in 1752, after thinking the matter over a long while, he decided that lightning must be the same thing as the electricity produced by rubbing a cat's fur. He therefore determined to bring lightning down from the clouds, to find out whether he was right. After many experiments, he built a kite, fastened a sharp point to it, and flew it one stormy day. He had taken all his measures so carefully that he thus really drew down some electric sparks from the sky.

As Franklin was a very practical man, he immediately made use of this knowledge to invent lightning rods for protecting churches and houses from thunderbolts. His discovery, ridiculed at first, soon became known abroad, and thus Franklin was the first American who won a European reputation.

Franklin's kite-flying paved the way for all the wonderful discoveries since made in electricity, many of which he then foretold, although people thought he was only joking. Indeed, we are told he even demonstrated the deadly effect of a live wire by killing a turkey on the other side of the river! When his discoveries became known in Europe, they created a great sensation, and the "Franklin experiments" were for a while all the fashion.

LV. BRADDOCK'S DEFEAT.

In 1754, Franklin, deputy postmaster-general of the colonies, was sent to Albany, where, as we have already seen, a congress of delegates from the colonies met to discuss the best way of opposing the French. Franklin, knowing that it was only by working all together that the best results could be reached, now made a plan for the union of the colonies.

As one can often make people understand things better by telling them stories or showing them pictures, Franklin remembered the common belief that a snake, cut into pieces, would become whole again if the parts were allowed to touch. He therefore placed at the head of his paper the picture of such a snake, cut into pieces to represent the colonies, which he further indicated by their initials. Under this picture he wrote the motto: "Join or die."

Although the colonies did not adopt Franklin's plan of union, they nevertheless voted men and money for the war. The British, on their part, sent over General Braddock, one of their best officers, to take charge of the campaign. Meeting the governors of the different colonies in Virginia, Braddock decided that, while one army marched north from Albany to take Forts Ti-con-der-o´ga and Crown Point before going on to Quebec, a second should move westward from the same point to Lake On-tä´ri-o and Niagara.

In the meantime, a fleet was to sail from New England to join the first army in besieging Quebec. But the fourth and principal expedition, led by Braddock himself, was to march across Pennsylvania to Fort Duquesne, so as to drive the French out of the coveted Ohio valley. This plan was very fine; but Braddock, used to the European way of fighting, little knew how to carry on war with the French and Indians in the pathless forests.

Washington now advised Braddock, his superior officer, to leave the heavy baggage and cannons behind; but the British general would not consent. After much delay, the Pennsylvania farmers loaned their wagons and horses to carry the baggage, thanks to Franklin's personal efforts, and the army set out. But as Braddock insisted upon the army's marching along in an orderly file, a road had first to be built, and Washington once impatiently said that they stopped "to level every molehill."

At Braddock's Defeat.

Washington knew it would be best to advance rapidly and surprise Fort Duquesne; but the army moved slowly until, at about eight miles from the fort, it was suddenly attacked by the French and Indians. The British soldiers, clad in red and marching in close ranks, made fine targets for their enemies, who, as usual, hid behind every tree and rock, whence they poured a deadly fire upon them. Braddock bravely rallied his men again and again; but not knowing how to fight unseen foes, they were helplessly slain. The general himself, after seeing great numbers of his men and officers fall, was mortally wounded, and had to order a retreat.

In the midst of this horrible scene, Washington and his Virginian soldiers alone kept cool. Four bullets passed through Washington's coat, and two horses were killed under him, for the Indians aimed specially at him. But all their bullets failed, and they afterwards said with awe that he surely bore a charmed life, and that no shot could ever touch him.

Nearly all the officers were killed, but Washington managed to cover the retreat of the British, and their wounded general was picked up and borne off the battlefield of the Mo-non-ga-he´la. Braddock was now full of remorse for not following Washington's advice, and he died four days later, saying: "Who would have thought it? Who would have thought it? We shall better know how to deal with them another time."

Washington sadly buried the brave general in the Pennsylvania woods, making the army march over his grave, so that no trace of upturned soil should betray to the Indians his last resting place. Then the beaten and disheartened troops slowly made their way back, encouraged by Washington, who, going afoot, shared all their hardships, and relieved the weary men by loading their muskets and baggage upon his own horse.

The army marching westward from Albany had, in the meantime, paused discouraged at Os-we´go, while the one moving northward beat the French on the shores of a lake, which they called George, in honor of the victory won for their king (1755). The French officer Dieskau (dees´kow) was captured there, and among the English dead was Ephraim Williams, who left his fortune to found the college in Massachusetts which bears his name.

Fearing that the Acadian farmers, who still spoke French and loved their mother country, would turn against them, the British now tried to make the peasants take an oath of fidelity. When they refused, the men and boys were bidden to assemble, and then, after some delay, they and their families were sent on board British ships and taken away (1755). In the confusion several families were separated.

Expulsion of the Acadians.

Thus ruthlessly torn from home, the Acadians were scattered throughout the colonies. Many made their way to Louisiana, so as to be still under French rule; others escaped into the woods; and a few spent long years vainly seeking those they loved. If you care to learn how one girl wandered thousands of miles in quest of her lover, you should read Long´fel-low's beautiful poem "E-van´ge-line."

LVI. WOLFE AT QUEBEC.

Until 1756, the war between the French and the British raged only in America; but after that it broke out in Europe also, where it was known as the "Seven Years' War."

The French sent over Mont-calm´, one of their best generals, who, helped by the Indians, soon took and burned Oswego. Next, he captured Fort William Henry, which the Americans had just built; but he promised that the garrison should leave under safe escort (1757). His Indian allies, however, loath to see the foe depart unharmed, suddenly attacked them, and killed many. Montcalm bravely and vainly tried to stop this, crying: "Kill me, but spare the English who are under my protection."

This year of 1757 was, on the whole, a disastrous one for the British; but during the next, the tables were turned. The principal statesman in England was then William Pitt, a good friend to the American colonies. Knowing that, unless prompt measures were taken, the British would lose the main part of their possessions in America, Pitt sent over men with great stores of arms and money.

The British and American troops, properly equipped, now started out again to carry out Braddock's plan. This time, Forbes was in command, ably assisted by Washington, and they forced the French to abandon Fort Duquesne. Near its ruins the British built a stockade which was named Pittsburg, in honor of William Pitt.

Upon returning to Virginia after this triumph, Washington, who had lately married a widow with two children, quietly took his seat in the House of Burgesses. To his dismay, the Speaker praised him for all he had done for his country. Embarrassed by this speech, Washington arose and vainly tried to make the proper response, until the Speaker, seeing his predicament, kindly said: "Sit down, Mr. Washington; your modesty equals your valor, and that surpasses the power of any language I possess."

A few months before the seizure of Fort Duquesne, the British captured the fortress of Louisburg for the second time, and Fort Frontenac was destroyed. Thus, step by step, the French were driven into Canada, where James Wolfe, a brave young British officer, was ordered to take Quebec. Now, Quebec is built upon a high rock, and it was impossible to reach its citadel from three sides. But Wolfe, thinking that it could be attacked from the Plains of A´bra-ham, went up the river past the city, and then, one night, drifted noiselessly downstream toward the place where he wished to land.

Wolfe was a charming young man, loving art and poetry, and as he went down the St. Lawrence, he mentioned a poem of Gray's, saying: "I would rather be the author of the 'Elegy Written in a Country Churchyard' than have the glory of beating the French to-morrow." Then he repeated the following lines with deep feeling:

"The boast of heraldry, the pomp of power,
And all that beauty, all that wealth e'er gave,
Await alike the inevitable hour;
The paths of glory lead but to the grave."

As the brave young man seemed to foresee, the path of glory was to lead him also to the grave. A few minutes later, his boats came within range of the French sentinels, and their challenge was answered in such good French that they let the boats pass. After landing, Wolfe climbed up the steep path, and had his army all drawn up for battle on the Plains of Abraham the next morning.

Battle of Quebec.

Montcalm, taken thus unawares, led out his troops and fought bravely; but he was defeated by Wolfe, who, as well as Montcalm, was mortally wounded in the fray. The French commander breathed his last a few hours later, saying: "Thank God, I shall not live to see Quebec surrender!"

His equally brave young enemy, dying on the battlefield, heard his men cry: "They run! they run!" Breathlessly he inquired, "Who run?" but when he heard that it was the French, he fell back, saying: "Now God be praised! I can die in peace."

This memorable battle, fought in 1759, is commemorated by a monument on the Plains of Abraham, on which the names of both generals are carved. There is also a famous monument in West´min-ster Abbey, in honor of Wolfe, the conqueror of Quebec.

The fall of Quebec decided the fate of the French in America. They had already lost the Ohio valley, Forts Ticonderoga and Crown Point, and soon after, Montreal surrendered too.

Although the last French and Indian War was now over in America, the war between France and England continued until 1763, when it was ended by the treaty of Păr´is. Because more land changed hands on this occasion than ever before, the treaty of Paris is known in history as the biggest land deal ever made. To Great Britain France gave up Canada and her claims to all the land east of the Mississippi, except New Orleans. For herself she kept only two small islands in the Gulf of St. Lawrence, on which to dry fish. Spain, siding with France in this war, received from her ally all of Louisiana west of the Mississippi, and the city of New Orleans. To recover Havana, which had been taken by a British fleet, Spain gave up Florida, which had belonged to her ever since Ponce de Leon first visited it in 1512.

Wolfe's Monument in Westminster Abbey.

All these changes did not please everybody, and the Indians so disliked the English rule that, led by Pon´ti-ac, one of their chiefs, they began a war which bears his name (1763). In the course of this struggle seven forts were taken, and many settlers cruelly slain.

The garrison at De-troit´, however, having been warned that the Indians were planning a surprise, showed so brave a front that Pontiac failed to get possession of that place. But some of his allies had better luck at Michilimackinac. They assembled near there as if to play a game, and tossing their ball nearer and nearer the palisade, finally made a wild dash through the open gates. The garrison was butchered, and only one trader managed to escape. Then, after continuing this war some time longer, the Indians were forced to submit, and three years later, Pontiac, the leader of the revolt, was shot by an Indian who had been bribed to kill him.

LVII. HOW ENGLAND TREATED HER COLONIES.

The people in England had seemed to think all along that the colonies in America ought to do all they could to enrich England. Their idea was that the mother country had a right to the earnings of the colonies, so they treated the colonists like little children, not old enough to think or work for themselves.

Among other things, the English made laws about trade and navigation which were very good for England, but very bad for the colonies. For instance, they said that the Americans should not sell their tobacco, rice, sugar, furs, etc., to any country except England. Any colonist having any of these things for sale had to put them on English ships, and pay freight to carry them to England. Then he had to pay duty before his produce could be sold. Some other articles could be sold to other countries, provided they were sent over in English ships. But no vessels from foreign countries were allowed to come into any of the American ports, either to buy or to sell; and if a colonist wanted something from France, he had to get it by way of England, although it cost him much more.

As if all this were not bad enough, the English were so anxious to sell the goods they manufactured, that they said the Americans must buy of them, instead of making such articles for sale. Thus, a farmer could hammer out rough tools for his own use from the iron dug up on his land, but he could not make even a hoe for his neighbors in any other colony.

Spinning.

The women, who spun and wove their own flax and wool, cut and made ordinary family garments, and plaited straw, which they sewed together for hats, could not even sell a pair of mittens in the next colony. If the New Englanders wanted to exchange codfish for Virginia tobacco, they either had to send it by way of England, thus paying for its being carried twice across the Atlantic, or else they were obliged to pay heavy duties.

In her fear that the colonies would sell to other countries anything she could use, England even forbade Americans to cut down any very large or straight trees without her permission. She said that all this timber should be kept until she needed it as masts for her vessels.

Of course, the colonies did not like this, but they bore it for a long time as patiently as they could. Other countries did not approve of England's trade and navigation laws, either. Both the French and the Dutch, for instance, wanted to trade with the colonies. As the coast was very long, and there were customhouse officers in only a few of the towns, some foreign vessels managed to slip into small bays unseen, and thus began smuggling goods in and out of the country.

As long as France owned Canada, smuggling could not very well be stopped, for French or Dutch vessels caught along the coast said that they were on their way to or from Canada, and that they had been driven out of their course by contrary winds. But when the last French and Indian War was over, foreign vessels no longer had any excuse for coming near North America. The British, therefore, declared they would now seize any foreign vessel they met, and search any house where they fancied smuggled goods could be found.

Orders to search houses were called search warrants. They gave government officers the right to go over every part of a dwelling, and look into every closet and drawer. But people like to feel that their houses are their own, and that no one can come in unless invited. Knowing that those search warrants would make it easy for any officer who happened to dislike them to annoy them constantly, the Americans naturally objected to them.

The man who first spoke publicly against these search warrants, in the old statehouse in Boston, was James O'tis. When he declared that this was not right, he was told it was done in Great Britain as well as in America. Otis then answered that, as the British had a share in making that law, they were, of course, obliged to obey it. But he added that the Americans had no seats in the British Par'lia-ment, had had no share in making the law, and were therefore not bound to respect it.

Many of the colonists agreed with Otis, so the British officers did not dare offend them by making frequent visits to their houses; but they kept ships along the coast to chase all suspicious vessels and see whether they had any foreign goods on board. This proceeding was almost as disagreeable to the colonists as searching their houses.

One of these boats, the *Gas'pee*, in pursuing a colonial vessel, ran ashore in Narragansett Bay, Rhode Island, in 1772. Before it could be worked off the shoal,—which is still known as Gaspee Point,—a number of the best citizens of Providence came in disguise and set fire to the ship. But although the British said their flag had been insulted, and tried to find the guilty parties, they never could lay hands upon them.

LVIII. THE STAMP TAX.

Besides the galling trade and navigation laws to which the poor American colonists had to submit, there were other troubles which you must try to understand. The French and Indian War had cost a great deal of money, which had to be paid. It was also needful to take steps to arrange for the government of the new territory, and especially to defend it, for the British knew that the French and Spaniards would like to get it back.

Now, King William's War, Queen Anne's War, and King George's War had been waged because England and France were fighting in Europe. They had done no good to the colonists, who, even after furnishing men and money, and winning Louisburg, saw it given back to the French. It was different, though, with the fourth war, which was begun in America, while Great Britain furnished men, money, and arms to defend the colonies. The colonies had done their best to help, and the American soldiers, whom the British mockingly called "Yankee Doodles," had shown great courage.

Franklin tried to arrange matters of taxation by his plan of government, which, you remember, was set aside at Albany (1754). The colonies refused it because they said it gave too much power to the king; and the king refused to accept it because it gave too much power to the colonies.

King George's advisers now told him that as Great Britain had run into debt fighting in America, it was only right that the colonies should help to pay the money. They added that it would be necessary to keep an army in America to defend the new-won lands, and that the colonies ought to feed and pay these soldiers.

If Great Britain had asked the colonies, "Will you support an army?" they might perhaps have consented. But instead of letting the Americans talk the matter over and raise the money in any way they pleased, measures were taken by Parliament to raise a large sum, which the king was to use in providing for a standing army.

At that time, many of the British were dissatisfied, too, for the members of the House of Commons no longer represented the whole nation. New cities like Bir´ming-ham, Man´ches-ter, and Leeds had no right to vote at all, while a few tumble-down places, which had been towns two hundred years before, still sent several members to Parliament. Pitt and some other statesmen said that a new census ought to be taken, and that the House of Commons should represent all the people of Great Britain; but the king, among others, thought things ought to remain just as they were.

The two parties were still quarreling over this when the question about America came up, and it was greatly because the British were not fairly represented that unjust laws were made. To raise the money, Parliament decreed that the colonies would have to keep the trade and navigation laws, and pay a tax upon sugar and molasses, and that no newspaper should be printed or deed written except on paper stamped by government officers. This was called the "Stamp Act."

As soon as Pitt heard that the Stamp Act had been passed, he said it was wrong to tax the colonies without their consent. But Parliament would not listen to him. In those days, vessels crossed the Atlantic only once a month. There was no telegraph, no daily newspapers, and the post between large cities like Philadelphia and New York ran only twice or thrice a week. It therefore took some time before the news of the passing of the Stamp Act became generally known in America.

Franklin, who was then in England, did his best to hinder the making of such an unjust law. He was once asked whether the Americans would be angry; and, hoping to make the British understand how unreasonable they were, he told them this story: A Frenchman once came running out of his house with a red-hot poker. He grasped an Englishman, passing by, and said: "Let me run this poker through you!" Of course the Englishman declined. Then the Frenchman said: "Well, let me at least run it a few inches into your body." But when the Englishman again refused, the Frenchman said, in an aggrieved way: "If you won't let me do either, you should at least pay for the trouble of heating this poker!"

Still, all Franklin's tact and good sense could not prevent the law being passed, and he sadly wrote home: "The sun of liberty is set; the Americans must light the lamp of industry and economy."

LIX. THE ANGER OF THE COLONIES.

Most Americans were not ready to take things so quietly as Franklin. Indeed, as soon as the news of the Stamp Act became known, there was great excitement. Bells were tolled, and every one looked sad. In Virginia, Patrick Henry arose in the House of Burgesses, and made a fiery speech which convinced the people that it would be wrong and cowardly to yield. In his speech he said that tyranny must be resisted, and added: "Cæsar had his Brutus, Charles I. his Cromwell, and George III.—" "Treason! Treason!" cried some of the members who were friends of the king. But Patrick Henry went firmly on, "may profit by their example. If this be treason, make the most of it!"

Patrick Henry's Speech.

His speech fairly carried the people away, and when he concluded it by saying: "Give me liberty, or give me death," the Virginians drew up a set of resolutions saying that they had the same rights as the people in Great Britain, that they could be taxed only by their assemblies, and that they would not allow any one else to tax them.

In North Carolina, John Ashe said: "This law will be resisted in blood and death." This opinion was so general that Massachusetts suggested that a general "Stamp Act Congress" should be held in New York, in 1765. All but four colonies were represented in it, and six of them drew up a paper saying that as British subjects they could be taxed only by their own consent, and that as they had no members in Parliament, they would not obey that body.

This paper was called the "Declaration of Rights," and they added to it another, saying that there were five things they had to complain about. These were: being taxed without their consent, being tried in some cases without a jury, being hampered in their trading, and being asked to pay the sugar tax and the stamp tax.

Men everywhere began thinking how they could keep their rights, and formed companies called "Sons of Liberty." These bands visited the men chosen to sell the stamped paper, and sternly warned them not to try to do so unless they wished to be treated like traitors. The result was that, so far as is now known, not a single sheet of stamped paper was ever sold in America. Indeed, when the day came when they were to have been first used, a Pennsylvania newspaper appeared with the heading, "No stamped paper to be had."

The excitement was such that even the children marched up and down like their elders, crying, "Liberty, Property, and No Stamps!" or even such hard words as "Taxation without representation is tyranny."

As we have already seen, there were many people in Great Britain who thought the Stamp Act unjust. Two great men, Burke and Pitt, openly said so; and when the news came that the Americans refused to obey, the latter exclaimed: "I rejoice that America has resisted. Three millions of people so dead to all the feelings of liberty as voluntarily to submit to be slaves, would have been fit instruments to make slaves of all the rest."

The British minister, Gren'ville, now sent for Franklin, and asked whether he thought the Americans would pay the stamp tax if it were less. But Franklin said: "No; never! They will never submit to it;" and went on to explain that it was not a question of more or less money, but a question of right and wrong.

As the Americans declared they would not buy a single thing from the British until their rights were respected, British vessels soon went home with unsold cargoes, and British merchants loudly cried that their business was ruined. These complaints, added to the colonists' determined resistance, made Parliament repeal, or call back, the Stamp Act, six months after it was to be enforced.

The stamps which were never used were stored away in a room in the House of Parliament. Here they lay forgotten for many a year, and when they were finally unearthed again, they were either given away as curiosities or destroyed.

The news of the repeal of the Stamp Act set the Americans almost crazy with joy. Bells were rung, bonfires lighted, and speeches made. In New York the people were so happy that they erected a new liberty pole, and made a big leaden statue of King George, which they set up on Bowling Green.

LX. THE BOSTON TEA PARTY.

In their joy the colonists did not at first notice that Parliament, in repealing the Stamp Act, still claimed the right to tax the colonies "in all cases whatsoever." But the very next year Parliament passed what are known in history as the "Townshend Acts," from the man who proposed them. These laws, besides forcing the colonists to feed the king's troops and keep the trade law, placed a tax on glass, paint, tea, and a few other things.

The money raised by these taxes was to be used partly for paying the salaries of governors, judges, customhouse and other colonial officers. Hitherto, the colonies had paid the salaries of governors and judges themselves, and they said that, while it might be all right to let a good king be paymaster, a bad king might make them very uncomfortable by sending out governors like Andros and Berkeley, who, being paid by him, would care only to please him.

Urged on by the Massachusetts people, all the colonies wrote to Great Britain that they would not buy any British goods until the taxes were removed. The king, offended by the letters sent him, ordered the governors to dissolve the colonial assemblies again and again; but he could not prevent the Americans from talking and thinking as they pleased. When his troops began to come, men, women, and children scowled at them, openly calling them "lobsters" and "bloody-backs" because they wore red coats.

As the Massachusetts people talked loudest, and urged the other colonies to resist, King George sent General Gage to Boston with two regiments. They came into the city on Sunday morning, with flags flying and drums beating, a thing which greatly shocked the good Puritans.

The "Boston Massacre".

The presence of British soldiers in America greatly annoyed the people. They daily grew more and more angry about it, and before long a small fight took place between soldiers and citizens, at Golden Hill, in the city of New York. Two months later, in the midst of the excitement caused by a false alarm of fire in Boston, a British soldier, annoyed by the taunts and snowballs of a mob, shot a man. This became the signal for more firing, which killed five men and wounded a few others (1770).

The excitement caused in the city by the "Boston Massacre," or the "Bloody Massacre," as it is known, in history, proved very great. Although the principal men in Boston knew the soldiers had not been greatly to blame for what had happened, they saw that there would be more trouble unless the troops left the town. Samuel Ad´ams, therefore, explained this to the governor, who asked him if the people would be satisfied if he sent one regiment away. Adams answered that he would find out, but, going to the Old South Meetinghouse, where the patriots were assembled, he passed up the aisle, whispering to his friends right and left: "Both regiments or none."

Faneuil Hall.

When Adams reached the platform, and told the people what the governor had said, his friends loudly cried: "Both regiments or none!" The rest of the people shouted the same thing. So the governor, much against his will, was forced to place the soldiers on an island in the bay. But after that, when mentioning those troops, King George spitefully called them "Sam Adams's regiments."

The removal of the soldiers quieted the Boston people a little; still, they often met in Faneuil (fan´el) Hall, where such stirring patriotic speeches were made that the building is often called the "Cradle of Liberty."

The people had said they would not buy anything from Great Britain until the taxes were removed; so, when tea ships came over, their cargoes were either sent back, stored in damp cellars, or destroyed. The British merchants complained about this, and the king himself, who was interested in the tea company, soon found he was losing money, too. He therefore proposed that the price of tea should be reduced, so that even after the tax of threepence a pound was paid, tea would be cheaper than ever before. But this made no difference to the colonists. The question with them was not cheap tea, but untaxed tea.

To prevent any one from buying any of this tea, all the ports were carefully watched; but finally three ships entered Boston harbor with strict orders to land their cargoes. As the governor would not send the ships back, and insisted that the king's orders should be carried out, Samuel Adams finally said, in a large assembly: "This meeting can do nothing more to save the country."

This was evidently a secret signal, for a voice immediately asked in an innocent way: "Will tea mix with sea water?" In reply some one shouted: "Boston harbor for a teapot to-night! Hurrah for Griffin's wharf!" The crowd now poured out of the Old South, and on reaching the street saw a band of men, disguised as Indians, rushing toward the pier. These make-believe Indians took possession of the dock, boarded the three ships, broke open the tea chests with their tomahawks, and poured their contents into the harbor, which thus became a monster teapot at Boston's famous Tea Party.

The Indians were careful, however, not to touch anything else, and when their work was done, they quickly vanished. Still, they were so honest that a padlock, broken by mistake, was secretly replaced by a new one on the next day. It is said that the tide the next morning left heaps of damp tea leaves on the beach. Some was put in bottles and kept, in memory of Boston's Tea Party; but the rest of it was either thrown back into the water or burned, so that no one should be tempted to touch it.

The Boston Tea Party.

LXI. THE MINUTEMEN.

Upon hearing the news of the Boston Tea Party Parliament made five harsh laws to punish the Bostonians. These were that no ships should be allowed to come in or go out of their port until they had paid for the tea; that the governor could send any one he pleased to England for trial; that the charter of Massachusetts was to be taken away; that the colonists should receive and feed the troops; and that the province of Quebec should be extended to the Ohio, thus including the western lands claimed by Massachusetts.

The Bostonians said they could not, and would not, stand these five laws, which they called the "five intolerable acts." The other colonies declared that the Bostonians were right, and promised to help them resist; so it was decided that delegates from all the colonies should meet at Philadelphia, in 1774, to act together.

All the colonies except Georgia sent delegates to this First Continental Congress. They met in Carpenter's Hall, in Philadelphia, and decided to print and circulate papers explaining to the colonies, to the Canadians, and to the British people their causes of complaint. They also drew up a declaration of rights and an address to the king.

Samuel Adams, who is often called the "Father of the Revolution," wrote this petition to the king; and his young daughter, seeing the paper, cried: "Only think of it; that paper will soon be in the king's hand!" But her father dryly answered: "My dear, it will more likely be spurned by the royal foot!"

PART OF THE NORTHERN STATES
COUNTRY AROUND BOSTON

There were many noted men among the fifty-five members of the First Continental Congress. Franklin had come home to take part in it, after having patiently tried to make peace with the Englishmen, who insulted him. While Congress was in session, some one asked Patrick Henry who was the leading man there, and he answered: "If you speak of eloquence, Mr. Rut'ledge of
South Carolina is by far the greatest orator; but if you speak of solid information, Colonel Washington is unquestionably the greatest man on the floor!"

Before separating, this congress decided that another should assemble the next year to hear King George's answer to their petition, and to discuss what steps should next be taken. But although Congress was dismissed, the colonies, in spite of the bad postal arrangements of the age, kept up a lively correspondence.

Patrick Henry, on his return home, told the Virginia convention what had been done, and concluded an eloquent speech by saying: "We must fight! I repeat it, sir, we must fight! An appeal to arms and the God of hosts is all that is left us." And in South Carolina the patriots loudly echoed the sentiments of their delegate, showing that "three million brave Americans, scattered over three thousand miles, had but one soul."

This was the opinion of patriots everywhere, and, feeling that they might soon be called upon to maintain their rights, they formed companies and drilled regularly. One of these bands of militia was formed in Virginia, where Washington said: "I shall very cheerfully accept the honor of commanding it, if occasion requires it to be drawn out." In New England many similar regiments were drilled, and as these volunteer soldiers were to be ready to start at a moment's notice, they were known as "minutemen."

The women were quite as patriotic as the men. They gave up tea and all other imported goods, and began to spin and weave with such energy that they and their families soon wore nothing but homespun. Even at a ball, in Virginia, the ladies wore rough cloth of their own manufacture, rather than purchase cloth, silk, and lace from England.

Statue of Minuteman.

As Boston suffered most of all, the other colonies showed their sympathy by sending all the supplies they could by land. Indeed, neighboring places, such as Mar-ble-head' and Salem, even offered to let Boston merchants use their port free of charge.

Instead of answering the "olive branch" petition sent by the colonies, King George told General Gage, governor of Massachusetts, to bring the people to order as soon as possible. But Gage soon saw that the colonists were too angry to yield tamely, and all he dared do was to stop their meetings and to fortify Boston Neck.

But meetings were held in spite of him, for the principal Bostonians went to Cambridge, where they formed a Committee of Safety. This was to watch the movements of the British, collect arms and ammunition, and see that the minutemen were always ready for duty. For every one now felt that the fight must soon break out, although neither party wished to begin it.

LXII. THE BATTLE OF LEXINGTON.

General Gage knew that the patriots were collecting supplies, and he was determined to seize them if he could. But there were good patriots in Boston who were watching him closely, and they had agreed to warn their friends of any danger, by means of lanterns hung up in the tower of the Old North Church.

Paul Revere's Ride.

Two lights in the tower, one night, notified the people of Charlestown that the British were moving, and the minutemen on guard scattered to rouse their fellow-soldiers. Paul Re-vere´, among others, dashed off on horseback, narrowly escaping capture by the British, who were guarding all the roads. As he galloped rapidly on, he roused the people by crying: "The British are coming!" Finally he reached Lex´ing-ton, about nine miles from Boston. Here Samuel Adams and John Hancock had both taken refuge, because Gage wanted to seize and ship them off to England, to be tried there for treason.

The clatter made by Revere roused the sleeping patriots, and when one of them asked what all this noise meant, Revere quickly answered: "Noise! You'll have noise enough before long. The regulars are coming!" Just then the window opened, and Hancock called Revere in. Soon after Revere rode rapidly on again to warn Concord, Massachusetts, while Adams began cleaning his gun to join in the fight. But Hancock stopped his companion, saying that it was their duty, as members of the Council, to plan and think, instead of fighting.

The alarm enabled the patriots to conceal most of their arms and stores, and when the British soldiers arrived in Lexington, soon after sunrise on April 19, 1775, they found about seventy minutemen drawn up on the green. The leader of the minutemen bade them "Stand firm! Don't fire until you are fired at. But if they want war, let it begin right here."

The British officer, at the head of about three hundred men, now loudly cried: "Disperse, ye rebels! Disperse!" Then, as they did not obey, he drew his pistols. Who fired first is a question which has never been settled, but a few minutes later seven American patriots lay on the ground dead, and the rest were obliged to retreat.

The British now marched on to Concord, where they began to destroy the stores. Although they had fancied the patriots would offer no more resistance, they soon found they were mistaken. The minutemen were assembling as fast as they could, and Dr. Warren addressed those at Lexington, saying: "Keep up a brave heart. They have begun it—that either party can do; and we'll end it—that only we can do."

The Retreat from Concord.

The British guard at the Concord bridge was now attacked. Hearing shots in that direction, the British hurried back, to find their men falling rapidly beneath the fire of the minutemen. The latter were posted behind every bush, tree, barn, and stone wall all along the road, so that the British had to retreat between two lines of fire.

Bewildered by the constant shots of enemies they could not see, the British soldiers soon broke ranks and rushed blindly on, never pausing to take breath until they met new forces at Lexington, which covered their retreat. There the fugitives fell to the ground exhausted and panting, their tongues hanging out of their mouths from heat and thirst. After they recovered a little, the British, who had marched out of Charlestown that morning playing "Yankee Doodle" to vex the patriots, were only too thankful to beat a retreat. When they reached their fortifications at sundown they had lost about three hundred men, while only eighty-eight of the patriots had fallen.

The Revolutionary War had begun, and the day after the battle of Lexington the Massachusetts Congress wrote to England: "We determine to die or be free." The news of the first bloodshed was rapidly carried from place to place by men on horseback. They went everywhere, calling the people to arms. Guns were polished and bullets cast, the women sacrificing even cherished pewter spoons and dishes to supply the necessary ammunition.

The call to arms found Israel Putnam—a hero of the last French and Indian War— plowing in his field. Unyoking his oxen from the plow, Putnam bade a lad run for his coat and gun, while he saddled his horse. He then rode quickly away to take part in the struggle, which was to last about seven years. Two other patriots, John Stark from New Hampshire, and Benedict Arnold from Connecticut, were equally prompt in responding to this appeal, and it is said that in less than three days, sixteen thousand Americans were assembled around Boston, completely hemming in General Gage and the British troops.

LXIII. BUNKER HILL.

The news of the battles at Lexington and Concord, where, as Em´er-son says, was "fired the shot heard round the world," traveled with remarkable speed to Ver-mont´. There the Green Mountain Boys quickly sprang to arms, and, under Ethan Allen, their leader, marched on to Fort Ticonderoga. This place was in the hands of the British, and contained large stores of arms and ammunition, which the Americans coveted.

But before the Green Mountain Boys reached Ticonderoga, Arnold joined them to assume command of their force. As Ethan Allen refused to give it up, the two patriots headed the force together. They came upon the fort so unexpectedly that, at the cry of "Surrender!" the British commander sprang out of bed and rushed to the door, defiantly asking, "By what authority?" "In the name of the great Jehovah and the Continental Congress!" thundered Ethan Allen. The British officer was forced to yield, although he knew the Green Mountain Boys could have no such orders, for the Second Continental Congress was to assemble only the next day. The taking of Ticonderoga, and of Crown Point on the morrow, proved a great help to the Revolutionary cause, for the patriots thus secured, cannon and powder which they were to need before long.

Traveling rapidly from place to place, the news of the battle of Lexington soon spread all through the colonies. The congressional delegates, therefore, left their homes to meet in Philadelphia, knowing there was a great piece of work before them. One of them, George Washington, felt it so keenly that before starting he wrote to his brother: "It is my full intention to devote my life and fortune to the cause we are engaged in, if needful."

It was well that he was so ready to serve his country, for it was sorely in need of help. Congress no sooner assembled, with Hancock for president, than it began to govern the country, and called for an army of fifteen thousand men. Adams then arose, saying he would like to propose as general a gentleman from Virginia, whose "skill and experience as an officer, independent fortune, great talents, and universal character will command the approval of all America."

George Washington, who had expected nothing of the sort, and who was as modest as he was good, fled from the room when he heard this. But every one voted for him, and when he was called back he reluctantly accepted the charge given him, saying: "I beg it may be remembered by every gentleman in this room that I this day declare, with the utmost sincerity, I do not think myself equal to the command I am honored with." But he then went on to say that he would do his best, and refused all pay for his services, asking only that Congress should pay his expenses, of which he would keep an exact account.

Washington wrote to his wife, at Mount Vernon: "I should enjoy more real happiness in one month with you at home than I have the most distant prospect of finding abroad, if my stay were seven times seven years." But as he always did his duty promptly and cheerfully, he immediately set out on horseback for Boston, where the continental troops were rapidly assembling.

The British, in the meantime, had withdrawn once more into Boston, which they duly fortified by earthworks across the Neck. Here they were soon joined by new troops; for Generals Howe, Bur-goyne´, and Clinton had been sent from England to put down the rebellion. On first hearing that the British soldiers were kept in Boston by ill-equipped and badly trained Americans, one of these officers cried: "What! can ten thousand Yankee Doodles shut up five thousand soldiers of the king? Only let us get in there, and we'll soon find elbow room!" But, as you will see, they did not find this an easy task.

The Americans, learning that the British were planning to fortify Bunker Hill and Breeds Hill, back of Charlestown, determined to prevent their doing so, if possible, by occupying those places first. Twelve hundred men were therefore put under command of Colonel Pres´cott, and, after a solemn prayer, they noiselessly crept up Breeds Hill in the darkness, and began to throw up earthworks.

As the patriots toiled silently on, they heard from time to time the British sentinels cry out, "All's well!" But when the sun rose, the British found that all was not well, for the Americans were intrenched on Breeds Hill. Still, thinking it would be an easy matter to dislodge the patriots, they joyfully prepared for the battle. The Americans did not quail when British bullets began to rain around them, for their leader, seeing their dismay when the first man fell, encouraged them by walking along the top of his breastwork as coolly as if there were no danger at all.

General Gage, perceiving him through his telescope, asked a Bostonian who he was, and whether he would fight. The Bostonian proudly answered that the man's name was William Prescott, and added: "Fight? Yes, yes! you may depend upon him to do that to the very last drop of blood in his veins." In the meantime, Prescott charged his men, who had few rounds of ammunition, not to fire until he bade them, or until they could see the whites of the enemies' eyes.

Battle of Bunker Hill.

This order was so manfully obeyed that when the redcoats climbed the hill they fell in swaths before the patriots' rifles. Twice the British fell back dismayed before this deadly fire, and twice their officers bravely rallied them and led them back. But Prescott kept up the courage of his men until, seeing that they had no more bullets, he bade them retreat, using their guns as clubs, since they had no bayonets. The gallant Warren, who had gone into this fight saying, "Sweet and fitting it is to die for one's country," fell on the very spot where Bunker Hill Monument how stands; and Prescott bravely covered the retreat of his men, being the last to leave the works.

Bunker Hill Monument.

In this battle, which is called the "battle of Bunker Hill," the British drove the patriots away, but at the cost of so many lives that when the news reached Europe a French statesman said: "Two more such victories, and England will have no army left in America." Not only did many British soldiers perish, but as the Americans discovered that the only cause of their defeat on this occasion was lack of ammunition, they looked forward to the next battle without fear.

All felt, as Ward said, that "We shall finally come off victorious, and triumph over the enemies of freedom and America." This belief, however, was not shared in England, although Franklin proved that it had cost the mother country three million pounds and many men to kill about three hundred and fifty Yankees. He added that in the meantime so many children had been born in our country that, at that rate, it would be impossible to find men and money enough to conquer the whole territory.

LXIV. THE BOSTON BOYS.

The news of the battle of Bunker Hill, and of Howe's setting fire to Charlestown during the struggle, was sent without delay to Congress. The messenger who bore it met Washington on his way to Cambridge to take command of the army. The general in chief eagerly asked how the Americans had behaved, and when he heard that they had stood their ground bravely, he fervently cried: "The liberties of the country are safe!"

The Cambridge Elm.

The messenger then continued on his way, and when the news reached Congress there was great excitement. The patriots felt that the fight could now end only when their rights were assured; and Franklin wrote to some friends in England: "England has lost her colonies forever."

Riding on, Washington quickly reached Cambridge, where he made his headquarters in the house later occupied by the famous American poet Longfellow. In the beginning of July, 1775, standing under the Cambridge Elm, Washington took command of the continental army, composed of about fifteen thousand men of every age and size. They were armed with hunting rifles, knives, swords, or pitchforks; most of them had no idea of military drill or discipline, and all were in need of arms, ammunition, uniforms, and food.

It was impossible to fight without three of these things; so while the patriots brought food for the soldiers, Washington bestirred himself to secure arms and ammunition, begging Congress to supply hunting shirts, so that his army might present a more orderly appearance. To prevent the enemy from discovering, through spies, that he had less than half a pound of powder for each man, Washington had a number of barrels filled with sand. A little powder was put on top of each, and they were stored away and guarded as carefully as if there were the greatest danger of their exploding at any minute.

While waiting for the artillery which Ethan Allen had secured at Ticonderoga to be brought across country on ox sleds, Washington and his aids drilled their ungainly troops. But the patriots were independent and hard to manage. It is said that when a corporal once bade a private get a pail of water, the latter coolly answered: "I won't. Get it yourself. I got the last pail; it is your turn now."

The officers, on the other hand, seemed afraid to lower themselves by doing any work. Washington, hearing a corporal urge his men to remove a log which was too heavy for them, suggested to the corporal that in such cases it was well to lend a hand. But the man proudly answered: "Do you realize that I am a corporal?" Feeling that example would be better than preaching, Washington dismounted, lent a vigorous hand to the men, and, when the log was in place, showed them his uniform and rode off, bidding the men call for him whenever they needed help.

Washington and the Corporal.

We are told that on another occasion he found some Marblehead fishermen and Virginia riflemen quarreling. Unable to bring them to order in any other way, Washington, who was more than six feet tall and very strong, strode into their midst, and, seizing the noisiest by their collars, shook them until he brought them back to their senses.

For eight months Washington waited and drilled, keeping the British shut up in Boston. Here the officers tried to kill time by writing and acting plays, and it is said that the most clever of all these productions was a work by An´dré making fun of Washington. The British soldiers, having nothing to do, annoyed the citizens, and so often spoiled the children's play on the Common, that a number of big boys finally went to General Gage to complain about it.

The British general angrily asked: "What! Have your fathers sent you here to exhibit the rebellion they have been teaching you?" But the boys bravely answered: "Nobody sent us. We have never injured your troops, but they have trampled down our snow hills and broken the ice of our skating pond. We complained, and they called us young rebels, and told us to help ourselves if we could. We told the captain, and he laughed at us. Yesterday our works were destroyed for the third time, and we will bear it no longer."

The boys' spirited reply could not but appeal to General Gage, who said to some people standing near him: "The very children draw in a love of liberty with the air they breathe." Then, turning to the boys, he added: "Go, my brave boys, and be assured that if my troops trouble you again they shall be punished."

LXV. THE BRITISH LEAVE BOSTON.

While Washington was holding the British prisoners in Boston, Congress made one more vain attempt to be on good terms with the king. But the only answer he made to their petition was to call for more soldiers. Finding that the English, who in many cases thought the Americans were right, would not fight for him, he hired seventeen thousand Hessian and other German soldiers to put down the rebellion.

The news that the king was hiring Germans and bribing the Indians on the frontier to make trouble, made the Americans very angry. On the same day, they heard that the British had burned down Fal´mŏuth (Portland), in Maine, so they determined to take active measures.

Knowing that the Ca-na´di-ans under Carle´ton would soon march southward, they sent two armies to the north. One, under Mont-gom´er-y, passed up Lake Champlain and soon took Montreal. The other army, although it was winter, heroically forced its way through the Maine woods to Quebec, led by Benedict Arnold.

There Montgomery joined Arnold; but their combined forces proved too weak to take the city. Montgomery fell in the very beginning of the fight, and Arnold, who had behaved like a hero, was badly wounded. Before he could recover and make a new attempt to seize Quebec,—where much ammunition was stored,—new British troops came and drove the American forces out of Canada.

Washington, as we have seen, was seemingly idle, only because his troops needed drilling and he had no powder. As he did not wish the enemy to know this, he kept the secret until many people began to murmur because he spent the winter in Cambridge with Mrs. Washington, without striking a blow. He had, however, been far from idle, for, besides drilling his army, he had made many arrangements, and provided that the American prisoners should be kindly treated or exchanged. To do this, he wrote to General Gates, who had fought by his side at Monongahela twenty years before, promising that the British prisoners should receive just the same care as was given to the Americans.

As soon as the cannons came from Ticonderoga, Washington resolved to attack Boston, in spite of the objections of his officers. The principal house owners there had long urged him to do so, notwithstanding the fact that their property would suffer greatly. One night, therefore, he bade his men secretly climb and fortify Dor'ches-ter Heights. When the British awoke the next morning, they saw that the American guns covered them. Rather than stand such a deadly fire, General Howe decided to leave the town. His troops, and about nine hundred of his friends, went on board the British vessels in the harbor, and sailed off to Hal'i-fax.

On St. Patrick's day, 1776, Washington triumphantly entered Boston, where his troops were received with every demonstration of great joy. Indeed, the Bostonians were so happy that they gave Washington a gold medal, on one side of which he is represented on horseback, pointing to the vanishing British fleet.

But Washington did not linger there long. Suspecting that Howe's next attempt would be to seize New York, and fearing lest he might have gone there straight from Boston, Washington soon hurried away. Just before he left the city, a British ship, laden with powder, sailed into the harbor, as its captain thought the British were still there. Its cargo was quickly seized, and provided the American army with seven times more powder than they had been able to secure by any other means.

About three months later a second British fleet, under Clinton, suddenly appeared off Charleston, where it began bombarding Fort Moultrie (moo'trī). The governor of Charleston having sent word to the general, "Keep cool and do mischief," the fire was promptly returned. Besides, the British were greatly dismayed to see their cannon balls burying themselves harmlessly in the soft palmetto logs and the big sand heaps of which the fort was composed. But the balls from the fort crippled the British vessels so badly that they had to sail away again without taking possession of Charleston.

In the midst of this battle, a British cannon ball cut Fort Moultrie's flagstaff in two, and brought down the flag. The enemy cheered loudly at this lucky shot; but a sergeant named Jasper quickly jumped over the parapet, caught up the fallen flag, and set it up again, notwithstanding the hail of bullets falling around him; so that it was now the Americans' turn to raise a cheer of triumph. In reward for his daring action, Jasper was offered the rank of lieutenant; but as he could neither read nor write, he sadly refused it, saying: "I am not fit for the company of officers."

LXVI. DECLARATION OF INDEPENDENCE.

In June, 1776, Richard Henry Lee brought into Congress a resolution "that these United Colonies are, and of right ought to be, free and independent States." This was now the opinion of the principal men in our country, and Washington wrote: "When I took command of the army, I abhorred the idea of independence; now I am convinced nothing else will save us."

John Trumbull, Artist.
Signing the Declaration of Independence.
The minds of the people having been prepared for the
change by a little pamphlet called "Common Sense," Congress appointed five men to draw up a Declaration of Independence. These five men were Thomas Jef´fer-son, Benjamin Franklin, John Adams, Roger Sherman, and Robert Liv´ing-ston; but as the paper, with the exception of a few words, is the work of Jefferson, he is generally called the "Father of the Declaration of Independence."

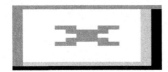

Jefferson's Writing Desk.
On July 4, 1776, this paper was adopted by Congress, after hours of discussion. In the meantime, crowds of people were anxiously waiting in the street in front of the old statehouse in Philadelphia to hear the decision of the Congress. A story says that the old bell ringer was at his post, ready to proclaim the glad news as soon as he received the signal from a grandson stationed below But time seemed so long to the old man that he muttered again and again: "They'll never do it." All at once, however, a little lad darted out of the statehouse, clapping his hands and shouting: "Ring, grandpa! Ring!"

Then the Independence Bell, which, strange to relate, bore the inscription, "Proclaim liberty throughout all the land unto all the inhabitants thereof," pealed out loud and clear, announcing the birth of the United States of America! All the other bells took up the joyful strain, and the news, flying from place to place, was welcomed everywhere.

John Hancock, president of Congress, was the first to sign the Declaration of Independence, writing his name in large, plain letters, and saying: "There; John Bull can read my name without spectacles. Now let him double the price on my head, for this is my defiance." Then he turned to the other members, and solemnly added: "We must be unanimous ; there must be no pulling different ways; we must all hang together."

"Yes," said Franklin, quaintly: "we must all hang together, or most assuredly we shall all hang separately."

We are told that Charles Carroll, thinking his writing looked shaky, added the words "of Carrollton," so that the king should not be able to make any mistake as to whose name stood there.

Pennsylvania Statehouse.

Copies of the Declaration of Independence were promptly sent to every colony, where it was solemnly read. In Pennsylvania this reading took place in the yard in front of the statehouse, which has ever since then been known as Independence Hall. It was there that the Liberty Bell hung, and pealed out the happy news. When the tidings reached New York, they were joyfully received by the army, and the Sons of Liberty pulled down King George's leaden statue. They later sent it to Connecticut, where patriot women broke it up and melted it to make bullets for the army.

At the same time, fault began to be found with the name of King's College, which had been established in New York over twenty years. But nothing was done till after the war, when the name was changed to Columbia College.

In the summer of 1776 Howe came into New York Bay with twenty-five thousand men, and soon after landed on Stat´en Island. In coming to New York, Howe was carrying out part of a great plan which had been made to separate the southern from the New England colonies. To do this, he was to march up the Hudson, while Carleton came south from Canada by way of Lake Champlain.

This plan was, as you see, very cleverly laid; but it was not so easy to carry out as the British expected. Although Carleton marched south and won a victory over Arnold at Valcour (val-coor´) Island, in Lake Champlain, it was at such a cost that he soon retreated in haste, instead of pressing on.

Soon after General Howe reached New York Bay, his brother, Lord Howe, made a proclamation offering pardon to all who would lay down their arms and promise to obey the king. Next, he sent an officer to the American camp, with this proclamation in a letter addressed to "George Washington, Esq." Washington, knowing that he must uphold the dignity of his country, rightly refused to receive any letter addressed to him as a private citizen. He said that George Washington, the Virginia planter, would not be at home to receive letters until the war was over, and that the general in chief of the American army could not receive any letters unless they bore the proper address.

Lord Howe now sent a second missive, addressed to "George Washington, Esq., etc., etc.;" but Washington also refused that. Seeing that the American general would not yield, Lord Howe ever after sent his letters properly directed, although he hated to do so, because it seemed to acknowledge the new government.

We are told that it was sometime during Washington's sojourn in New York that the British bribed a man to throw poison into the general's dish of pease. But, thanks to the warning of a faithful servant, Washington, although very fond of them, did not eat any, and thus escaped death.

LXVII. A LADY'S WAY OF HELPING.

While Washington was in New York, Putnam had charge of the troops on Long Island. Here General Howe suddenly came upon him with such a large force that Putnam was beaten and forced to retreat. Washington, who saw the battle of Long Island from a distance, is reported to have wrung his hands, and to have cried, with tears running down his cheeks: "My God! what brave fellows I must lose this day!"

At nightfall, the Americans were intrenched on Brooklyn Heights, where Howe planned to take the "nest of rebels" by siege. But, thanks to a fog which rose over the bay,

Washington cleverly and noiselessly drew off these troops, and when the sun rose on the second day, Howe found that the Americans were all on the other side of the East River. Knowing that Howe would pursue him, and not wishing to expose New York city to the enemy's cannon, Washington began to retreat up the Hudson.

While part of the British army landed near the Battery, the rest, under Howe himself, crossed the East River higher up, so as to cut off the retreat of the Americans under Putnam. To prevent this, Washington stationed troops at the landing at Kips Bay (where East Thirty-fourth Street now ends), bidding them hold the British at bay long enough to enable Putnam to retreat. But the Americans fled at the first fire, although Washington tried to stop them. In his rage and despair over their cowardice, Washington is said to have flung his hat on the ground, and bitterly cried: "Are these the men with whom I am to defend America?"

Still, one man could not hold an army in check; so Washington rode northward, sending word to Putnam to hurry, and begging Mrs. Murray, a lady living on a hill near by, to use her woman's wit to detain the enemy. Mrs. Murray bade her servants prepare refreshments, and when General Howe rode past her gate, she stepped out to invite him into her house.

It was a very warm day, the house looked cool and inviting, and Howe accepted, thinking a few moments' delay would not do any harm. But the ladies proved so entertaining, and the food they set before the officers so welcome, that instead of staying only a few moments, they lingered there several hours. Finally a servant came in and whispered something to Mrs. Murray, who, rising from her seat, begged Howe to accompany her to see something which she thought might interest him.

Hale statue

We are told that she then led the British general to an upper window, and pointed out Putnam's army vanishing in the dim distance. The delay had enabled the Americans to escape to a point higher up, where they still held Forts Lee and Washington, on either side of the river.

While the battle of Long Island was raging, Washington, needing information, sent Nathan Hale, a Yale graduate, into the British ranks. This brave youth was betrayed by a former friend, and the British, having taken him captive, condemned him to be hanged as a spy. This was no more than the young man expected; but they cruelly refused him a Bible or a minister to prepare for death.

We are told that even his last letters to his mother and betrothed were torn to pieces before his eyes, as they dragged him off to the gallows. But as the young patriot stood there, surrounded by foes, he firmly said: "I regret only that I have but one life to lose for my country." These noble words are carved on the pedestal of his statue, which now stands in one of the principal squares of New York city.

Howe and Clinton were now both in New York, where they were warmly welcomed by a few persons who were still faithful to King George. But as they had failed to secure the American army, they soon set out to pursue Washington, who slowly retreated before them.

Washington did not try to do more than check their advance, because he knew their ships could sail up the Hudson, across which he had vainly tried to make a barrier by sinking some old ships. Step by step, therefore, Washington withdrew until he came to White Plains. There a battle was fought; but, while the Americans were defeated, the British retreated on the next day, rather than renew the fight and lose more men.

Washington had left General Nathanael Greene in charge of Fort Washington, telling him to forsake it rather than run any risk of losing his troops. But Greene thought it would be safe to remain there awhile longer. Unfortunately, however, a traitor gave General Howe the plans of the place, thus enabling him to surprise and capture Fort Washington, together with three thousand men.

These soldiers, like many other American prisoners, were sent on board a rotting ship in New York harbor, where, in the course of the Revolutionary War, more than eleven thousand men died from bad food, bad water, and bad air. These victims of British cruelty were first buried in the mud at low tide, but their remains now rest in Washington Park, Brooklyn. A memorial monument has also been erected in their honor in Trinity Church, bearing the inscription: "To those great and good men who died while imprisoned in this city, for their devotion to the cause of American Independence." This honor was well deserved, for soldiers who die of disease or in captivity are just as likely to be heroes as those who fall on the battlefield.

Washington, seeing his fort taken, now went to Hack´en-sack, sending orders to General Charles Lee to cross the Hudson and join him in New Jersey. But instead of obeying promptly, Lee delayed so long that, as you will soon see, he hampered Washington greatly. The British, in the meantime, crossed the river, and Greene was obliged to leave Fort Lee in hot haste. Indeed, the enemy were so near that they found the soup pots still boiling on the fire, and merrily ate the dinner which was to have been served for the Americans.

Still faithful to his plan to worry and check the British, without meeting them in open battle, Washington now slowly retreated across New Jersey. We are told that he often left a place as the enemy came in; and because he thus imitated the tactics of a Roman general, you will often hear him called the "American Fā´bi-us."

Corn-wal´lis, the British general now in charge, pursued the Americans as fast as he could, in order to force them to meet him in pitched battles. But while the armies were often close enough to hear the music of each other's bands, and there were many small skirmishes, no real battle took place.

In one of these small engagements the wads used in loading the guns gave out. The chaplain of the regiment, who hated the British because they had cruelly shot his wife and baby, rushed into a church, tore up some hymn books, and, carrying the leaves to the soldiers for wads, said: "Give 'em Watts, boys! Give 'em Watts!"

LXVIII. CHRISTMAS EVE.

While retreating before Cornwallis, Washington kept sending stern orders to Lee to hasten and join him, so that their combined forces could be used against the British. But Lee did not obey, and came on very slowly. Indeed, he said freely that he did not consider Washington a good general, and often boasted that if *he* were only at the head of the army the war would soon be over.

Lee was in a little inn in New Jersey, writing a letter to General Gates expressing his opinion of Washington, when he was suddenly surrounded by the British and made a prisoner. Without giving him time to change his dressing-gown and slippers, or get into his uniform, the British bore him off in triumph, thinking they had taken the most clever of all the American generals. But Lee was really no loss, and his army, having fortunately gone on ahead, joined Washington sooner without a general than it would have done had Lee been there.

Many of the Americans now fancied, like the British, that since Lee was a prisoner their mainstay was gone. Besides, the British began to threaten to illtreat Lee, and as the Americans held no British generals as prisoners, they could not offer an exchange. Knowing this, a Rhode Island officer named Barton made a bold plan.

He had heard that the British General Prescott was quartered on the seashore not very far from Newport. Taking a party of forty brave seamen and soldiers, he rowed with muffled oars right through the British fleet, one dark night. Then a sentinel was noiselessly killed, and the small force surrounded the house where Prescott lay asleep. A moment later the Americans burst into his bedroom, bore him off half clothed to their boats, and, rowing away in safety, sent word to the British that Prescott should receive just the same treatment that they gave Lee. Nine months later an exchange was made, and Lee and Prescott went back to their posts (1778).

In the meantime Washington still avoided a battle, and retreated to the Delaware. There, having cleverly secured every boat within a hundred miles, he took his army over the river. When the British came up, not a single boat was to be had; so they camped near the stream, thinking it would soon freeze hard enough to allow them to cross on the ice and seize Philadelphia.

This was a time of great trial for the Americans, and Washington was the only man who did not despair. Still, the British had set a price upon his head, and were loudly boasting that they would soon hang him. Speaking of this, Washington once told his friend Joseph Reed: "My neck does not feel as though it were made for a halter." Then he added that if things came to the worst they would have to retreat into Virginia, or even over the Alleghanies, but that they must never give up the struggle they had begun.

Congress, fearing the British would carry out their plan and seize Philadelphia, now hastily withdrew to Baltimore. But before leaving, Samuel Adams wrote: "Let America exert her own strength, and He who cannot be indifferent to her righteous cause will even work miracles, if necessary, to establish her feet upon a rock."

Washington, as we have seen, was very prudent; but he was not lacking in courage. Seeing that the British forces were scattered, he now thought it a fine chance to win a victory, which would rekindle the ardor of his men and give new courage to all the nation.

Emanuel Leutze, Artist.

Washington crossing the Delaware.

He therefore planned to surprise the Hessians at Trenton by crossing the river, in spite of huge cakes of floating ice which nearly blocked it. Marblehead fishermen were put in charge of the boats, and such was their skill and daring that they took twenty-four hundred men safely over. This crossing of the Delaware on Christmas night (1776) was one of the most daring feats ever performed. Besides, the men were only half clad, and so badly shod that they left bloody footprints in the snow; and the cold was so intense that night, that two of their number were actually frozen to death.

In spite of drifting snow and driving wind, Washington's force marched bravely on, and surprised the Hessians at Trenton. The wounded commander, Rahl, was forced to surrender, and his whole army was seized. We are told that the Hessian soldiers had been so busy keeping Christmas that they were all half drunk, and that Rahl himself was too absorbed in a game of cards to read a note sent to warn him of his peril. Thinking it a matter of no importance, he thrust it into his pocket unread, and thus he and his men fell into Washington's hands.

The news of the victory of Trenton filled the hearts of the Americans with great joy, but it proved a bitter disappointment to Cornwallis. Fancying the war all over, he had packed his trunks and gone on board a vessel to return to England. But now General Howe sent him back in haste to Trenton to fight Washington. Hedged in between a river full of floating ice and a large army, it now seemed as if Washington could not escape.

One evening, therefore, Cornwallis gleefully told one of his officers that they would "bag the old fox" on the next day. The officer suggested that it might be better not to postpone it till the morrow; but Cornwallis answered that this time the Americans could not escape. That same night, however, Washington took advantage of the fact that the roads froze hard enough to enable him to remove his cannon, and slipped away by back roads, leaving his camp fires burning brightly so as to deceive the enemy. When the British awoke the next morning, the "old fox" was gone, and sounds of firing in the direction of Prince′ton soon convinced them that a battle must be going on there.

Running into Cornwallis's tent, an officer roused him, crying: "To arms, general! Washington has outgeneraled us. Let us fly to the rescue of Princeton!" But, notwithstanding all their haste, they reached Princeton only after the battle—on the present college grounds—was all over, and the victorious Washington had safely advanced to Mor′ris-town Heights. This campaign, in the dead of winter, was so wonderful that it won for Washington the title of "Savior of his Country," and Frederick the Great of Prussia once said that it was the most brilliant piece of generalship in the pages of history.

LXIX. THE FIGHT AT BENNINGTON.

While Washington was spending the rest of the winter at Morristown, the news of his triumphs reached France. Franklin had been sent there, in 1776, to secure help, if possible. His reputation as a man of science, his great talents, and his affable manners made him a great favorite in Paris, where the fashionable ladies and gentlemen carried fans and snuffboxes decorated with his portrait. But although both king and queen received Franklin very graciously, they would not at first promise him any aid.

A young French nobleman named La-fä-yette′, longing to help the Americans, now decided to leave his young wife and home. But as the king forbade him to leave court, he secretly embarked upon a vessel he fitted out himself, and crossed the Atlantic. Then, as soon as he landed, he went straight to Congress and offered to serve the United States without pay. A few days later he met Washington, whose helper he became, and who soon learned to love him as dearly as if he had been his own son.

Washington and Lafayette.

Several other illustrious foreigners came in the same way to fight for America and freedom. The bravest among them were the Germans De Kalb′ and Steu′ben, and the Poles Pu-las′kĭ and Kos-ci-us′ko. It is said that when Kosciusko first presented himself, and was asked what he could do, he briefly answered: "Try me." This reply so pleased Washington that he made the young man his aid-de-camp.

Washington's victories at Trenton and Princeton, and his return toward New York, could not divert Howe from his purpose to secure Philadelphia. When summer came on, therefore, he set out with his fleet to take that city. Washington began retracing his steps, and, knowing that Howe could not sail up the Delaware,—which was defended by forts,—went to meet him at Chadds Ford on the Bran'dy-wine (1777). Here a battle was fought, and not only were the Americans defeated, but Lafayette was sorely wounded.

Although beaten, Washington's army retreated in good order to Philadelphia, which was soon taken by Howe and the British forces. Hoping to drive them away, Washington surprised them, one morning, at Germantown. Here he would have won a brilliant victory, had not a dense fog made two divisions of his men shoot each other before they discovered their mistake, thus creating a panic.

As there was nothing to be gained by fighting with exhausted troops, Washington now withdrew, and before long went to Valley Forge for the winter. Meanwhile, Howe attacked the forts on either side of the Delaware River. One of these held out bravely for six days, refusing to surrender until it had been battered to pieces. Then, as one fort alone could not check the British fleet, the second surrendered also.

Hoping to damage some of the British vessels at Philadelphia, the patriots made rude torpedoes, which were placed inside of small kegs and sent floating down the river. One of these engines struck a cake of ice and exploded, and the British, thus warned of danger, shot at every floating object they saw, thus waging what has been called in fun the "Battle of the Kegs."

The British, having nothing else to do, now settled down comfortably in Philadelphia, where they lived on the very best of everything. They spent most of their time giving balls and parties, and grew so fat and lazy that, as Franklin wittily said, "Howe has not taken Philadelphia so much as Philadelphia has taken Howe." This remark proved true, for although the plan had been that Howe should march northward, he was delayed by Washington until it was almost too late. Besides, we are told that the British general never received positive orders to go north, for the paper, being badly written, was laid aside to be copied, and forgotten until too late.

Meanwhile the British again tried to carry out their plan of invading New York from Canada. This time, while one army started from Lake Ontario for the Mo'hawk valley, Burgoyne came southward up Lake Champlain, with British and Indian troops, and took Forts Ticonderoga and Edward. This was considered a great victory in England, and when King George heard that Ticonderoga was taken, he clapped his hands and shouted: "I have beat them! I have beat all the Americans!"

This was not true, however. But General Schuy'ler, sent to oppose Burgoyne, had so small a force that all he could do was to hinder the enemy's advance by cutting down trees and destroying bridges.

The king's advisers had told Burgoyne to hire Indians to help him, and in spite of all he could do to prevent it, these savage allies fought with their usual cruelty. They even killed and scalped Jane McCreā, a beautiful young lady, who, it is said, was on her way to meet a British officer to whom she was engaged. When this man saw her long golden locks among the scalps the Indians brought back, he left the army, and spent the rest of his life alone, mourning for his betrothed.

After taking the two forts, Burgoyne, hearing that there were cannon and stores at Ben'ning-ton, Vermont, sent part of his German troops thither to secure them. But when his men drew near this place, they found it ably defended by General Stark.

Even as a boy, this American patriot had always shown great courage and presence of mind. Once, when a prisoner of the Indians, and forced to run the gantlet. Stark snatched a club from one of his captors, and struck right and left with such vigor that he dealt more blows than he received. Later on, he also did many brave deeds during the French and Indian wars.

When the Germans drew near Bennington, Stark led his men against the foe, crying: "There they are, boys! We beat them to-day or Molly Stark's a widow." The men, fired by his example, fought so bravely that they soon won a signal victory. As Washington said, this was a "grand stroke," for the Germans were almost all captured or killed, while only a few of the Americans were lost.

We are told that one old man had five sons in this battle. On the morrow, a neighbor, wishing to break the news of one son's death, gently said: "One of your sons has been unfortunate." "Did he run away or neglect his duty?" the father asked quickly. "No; worse than that! He has fallen, but while fighting bravely." "Ah!" said the father, "then I am satisfied!" For the old man was such a good patriot that he was quite willing his sons should die for their country, and considered that only traitors and cowards needed pity.

LXX. BURGOYNE'S SURRENDER.

The victory at Bennington not only saved the American cannon and supplies from the hands of the foe, but enabled Stark and the Green Mountain Boys to get between Burgoyne and Canada. They thus cut him off from all help from the north, whence he expected both food and ammunition for his men.

While Burgoyne was thus between Generals Schuyler and Stark, St. Lĕǵ´er, another British general, was coming along the Mohawk valley to join Burgoyne at Albany. On his way, however, he stopped to besiege Fort Stan´wix, or Schuyler. Eight hundred volunteers set out to reinforce the garrison, but on the way thither, at O-ris´ka-ny, they were surprised by the Indian chief Brant. Their leader, General Her´ki-mer, mortally wounded in the very beginning of the engagement, bade his men place him under a tree, and then bravely said: "Now, go and fight. I will face the enemy." In spite of pain, he calmly lighted his pipe, and, while smoking, directed his troops with such vigor that before long the Indians were routed.

The garrison at Fort Stanwix, hearing shots in the forest, made a brave sortie, in which they captured five flags from St. Leger. These they hoisted above their fort, upside down, putting above them all a new flag made from pieces of a soldier's old shirt, a blue jacket, and a red flannel petticoat. Although fashioned from such queer materials, this flag bore thirteen alternate red and white stripes, and in a blue field in one corner was a wreath of thirteen white stars, the number of the United States. This was the new American flag suggested by Washington—whose coat of arms bore stars and stripes—and adopted by Congress in June, 1777.

But while the patriots thus fashioned a rude flag in the wilderness, and were the first to fight under this emblem, it was Mrs. Ross, of Philadelphia, who made the first American flag of this kind, in June, 1777.

When Schuyler heard of Herkimer's brave stand, and of the bold sortie from Fort Stanwix, he bade Arnold go and relieve the fort. Fearing that his force might not prove strong enough, Arnold made use of a trick. He told one of the prisoners, a half-witted lad, that he should be free if he would only do exactly as he was bidden. The lad agreed, and, clad in torn garments, ran to St. Leger's camp, loudly shouting, "The Americans are coming!" Of course the British and Indians crowded around him, and when the idiot was asked how many men were on the way, he answered by pointing mysteriously to the leaves on the trees overhead. This strange behavior made St. Leger believe that a large force was advancing, and created such a panic among his men that, in spite of all he could do, they beat a hasty retreat.

As St. Leger had gone back, and Howe had not come up the Hudson, Burgoyne was left entirely alone in the heart of the enemy's country. Schuyler was therefore on the point of winning a glorious victory, after all his hard work, when Congress suddenly bade him give up his command to General Gates. Although wounded to the quick by this order, Schuyler was too noble a man to show any anger. He gallantly said, "The country before everything," and asked permission of Gates to serve as an officer under him, since he could no longer command.

Burgoyne was surrounded, and seeing that he must fight, he advanced toward the American position on Be´mis Heights, near which the first battle of Săr-a-tō´ga took place. But night came on before it was over, and for more than two weeks the armies stood face to face, watching each other closely, yet not daring to risk a new battle. Finally, seeing that he must fight, starve, or retreat, Burgoyne marched out again, to face the Americans in what is known as the battle of Still´wa-ter.

Daniel Morgan and his sharpshooters, posted behind trees, carefully singled out the bravest men, and shot them with unerring aim. Indeed, such was their skill that it is said Morgan's riflemen could "toss up an apple and shoot all the seeds out of it as it fell."

Chief among the British officers on that day was General Fra´ser, who, when urged to take a less exposed position, simply replied: "My duty forbids me to fly from danger." Even while he was speaking thus, Morgan pointed him out to one of his best marksmen, saying: "That gallant officer is General Fraser. I admire and honor him; but he must die. Stand among those bushes, and do your duty." These orders were so promptly carried out that a moment later Fraser lay among the dead.

Arnold had been unjustly deprived of his command, but he could not keep out of the fray. Dashing to the front, he led the advance with his usual bravery, and forced his way into the British camp. But as he reached it he fell wounded in the same leg which had suffered at Quebec. His men tenderly bore him off the field of battle, where he had won a victory while General Gates was lingering in his tent.

During the battle, some women and children who were with the British army crouched in terror in the cellar of a neighboring house, listening to the shriek of the cannon balls overhead. The wounded in this building clamored for water, until, knowing the men would perish if they ventured out, a soldier's wife marched boldly down to the river. She did this several times, in full view of the Americans, who admired her courage and let her alone.

The battle had raged so fiercely that Burgoyne retreated to Saratoga, where he held a council of war to determine whether he should surrender. In the midst of his talk, an eighteen-pound cannon ball passed right over the table where he and his officers sat, so they quickly and wisely concluded that it was high time to give up (1777). The British soldiers, therefore, laid down their arms, and the Americans marched into their camp playing "Yankee Doodle," the tune they had adopted as a national air.

We are told that Burgoyne, on handing Gates his sword in token of surrender, proudly remarked: "The fortune of war, General Gates, has made me your prisoner"; to which Gates answered, as he gave it back: "I shall always be ready to bear testimony that it has not been through any fault of your Excellency." Later on, touched by the courtesy of Schuyler, whose house he had burned down, Burgoyne said: "You show me much kindness, though I have done you much injury." "That was the fate of war," said Schuyler, kindly; "let us say no more about it."

Burgoyne's Surrender.

LXXI. THE WINTER AT VALLEY FORGE.

Although Gates received all the credit at first, the two battles of Saratoga were really won by Schuyler, Morgan, and Arnold. Burgoyne's surrender proved the turning point of the Revolutionary War, so the fight at Saratoga is known as one of the decisive battles of the world. Not only did it end the British plan of separating New England from the Southern States, but it made the French promise to help the Americans openly. It also gave King George such a fright that he even offered to let the Americans send members to Parliament, if they would lay down their arms and promise to obey him.

But this offer, which would have more than satisfied the colonists a short time before, came too late. They had suffered so much that they were not willing to give up what they had won and again become subject to a king who, like those who had come before him, might at any time change his mind or break his promises. Besides, they remembered only too clearly that, after granting charters, kings had often taken them away again, and so they decided to keep on fighting until the matter was settled once for all.

The news of the victory at Saratoga created a great sensation in Paris, where the French had been waiting to see how things turned out before they openly sided with the Americans. The king now not only acknowledged the independence of the United Colonies of America (1778), but made a treaty of friendship and commerce with them, and soon sent a fleet to help them fight the British.

This happy turn of affairs was mainly brought about by Franklin, who for the past two years had been making as many friends for America as he could. Every one admired him for his learning and good nature, and the French minister Turgot (tur-go´) once proposed his health, saying: "He snatched a thunderbolt from heaven, and the scepter from the hand of the tyrant!"

But Franklin—who had a keen sense of humor, and, like all really great men, was very modest—smiled, and quaintly answered that while he appreciated the kindness of the speech, he was obliged to confess that not only had he left thunder in the clouds,—just where he had found it,—but that more than one million of his countrymen had helped him snatch the scepter from the hands of the tyrant!

News traveled so slowly in those days that it took months before Franklin heard of Burgoyne's surrender, and before Washington and Howe received word that the French were going to help the colonies openly. These months were full of hardships for all the Americans, for while the men were away fighting, the heroic women were obliged to do their work too.

At Valley Forge.

Washington's army, as we have seen, had encamped at Valley Forge, where the soldiers lived in rude log huts. They were without proper food or clothes, and cowered miserably over camp fires, for which they had to carry wood on their backs from neighboring forests. Even General Washington had but one room, and lived on cabbage and potatoes, with a few hickory nuts for dessert from time to time.

His heart was wrung at the sight of his men's sufferings, and as soon as his wife joined him at Valley Forge, he begged her to work as hard as she could to supply the men with stockings. Mrs. Washington's own knitting needles now flew faster than ever; besides, she interested all her friends in the work, and every day visited the soldiers' quarters, carrying them the stout garments thus secured. But provisions grew so scarce that Washington had to send all the women home, and Mrs. Washington again withdrew to Mount Vernon, where she lived as economically as possible, working day and night for her husband and the army.

As if matters were not bad enough already, some of the officers now formed a plot to take the command away from Washington, and put Gates at the head of the army in his stead. This plot, known as the Conway cabal, was headed by a man named Conway, to whom Washington had been particularly kind, but who was angry because he had not been promoted as fast as he wished.

The question was brought before Congress at Baltimore, where, hearing that there was danger of Washington's being dismissed for lack of a vote, Du´er, one of his friends, although ill in bed, determined to go to the meeting. His doctor, however, said that if he did so it would be at the risk of his life. "Do you mean I should expire before reaching the place?" asked Duer. "No; but I should not answer for your leaving it alive," answered the doctor. Hearing this, the good man firmly said: "Very well, sir; you have done your duty; now I will do mine." Then he called for a litter to carry him to Congress.

Luckily for him, some of Washington's friends came back in time to prevent his leaving his sick room. But better still for the welfare of our country, the Conway plot failed, and Washington remained at the head of the army. Conway had been so ungrateful that he was forced to leave the country, where people despised him for the mean part he had played.

All these trials wrung Washington's noble heart, and as he had no privacy in his headquarters, he sometimes rode out alone to think. A Quaker, hearing a noise in the bushes, once stole up cautiously, and found the general's horse tied to a tree. A few feet farther away, he beheld Washington kneeling in the snow, praying aloud for his country, with great tears streaming down his cheeks. The good Quaker crept away again unseen, but in telling the story some years later, he remarked that he felt at the time that the Lord could not but answer the fervent prayer of so good a man.

LXXII. THE QUAKER WOMAN.

The British quartered in Philadelphia were leading an easy and merry life; but several times during the winter Howe made plans to surprise Washington's troops. To his dismay, however, his plans always seemed known to the Americans, and therefore failed. Afraid that some spy might overhear him, Howe once held a secret meeting at night in the house of a Quaker woman, named Lydia Darrah. To make sure that he should not be overheard, he bade her go to bed, and see that all her family retired likewise.

Lydia obeyed, and the general, thinking all was safe, explained his plan to his officers. But the Quaker woman had noiselessly slipped out of her room again, and was now standing at the door listening to all that was said. As soon as the talk was over she crept back to her room, and when the officers had all gone, Howe called her, as agreed, to lock the door behind him. But she pretended to be sound asleep, and let him knock at her door three times before she rose, yawning, to show him out.

The next day, Lydia, who had not dared breathe a word of what she had heard to any one, said she was out of flour, and got a pass to go and buy some at a village near by. Meeting a patriot there, she quickly warned him of Washington's peril, and then quietly went home.

The next day Howe crossly said to her: "It is very strange; you, I know, were asleep, for I knocked at your door three times before you heard me; yet it is certain we were betrayed. On arriving, we found Washington so prepared at every point that we have been compelled to march back without injuring our enemy, like a parcel of fools." Lydia heard this without making a sign, and not till the war was over did it become known that it was she who had saved the army.

Besides the American patriots, foreigners were helping Washington with all their might. Among these was the Prussian officer, Baron Steuben, who knew no English, and therefore brought over an interpreter with him. According to one story, this interpreter made an idle bet to kiss the first Yankee girl he met. Landing at Portsmouth, this man won his wager by stepping up to a pretty girl, bowing politely, and begging permission to kiss her, saying: "Before leaving my native land to fight for American freedom, I made a vow to ask, in earnest of victory, a kiss from the first lady I should meet." The story adds that the young lady accepted the kiss, saying she could not refuse so small a favor to a man who had come to fight, and if necessary, to die, for her country.

Steuben joined Washington at Valley Forge, and there began to drill the troops, so they could meet the British on an equal footing. At first the German officer was shocked by their lack of discipline, and swore at them in every language he knew; sometimes he even called to his interpreter: "Come and swear for me in English; these fellows will not do what I bid them."

You see, soldiers in those days thought it manly to swear; and as Baron Steuben had been accustomed to European soldiers, who obeyed without a question, it took him some time to grow used to Americans, who, as he said, had to be told, "This is the reason why you ought to do that," before they would obey. Still, he soon taught our men to fight like old and trained soldiers.

The winter the troops spent at Valley Forge was one of the coldest ever seen, and therefore the soldiers' sufferings were very great. But with the spring, hope revived, for the news of the coming French fleet made the British leave Philadelphia to defend New York.

General Howe having gone back to England for his health, it was Clinton who conducted this retreat. Leaving the camp at Valley Forge, Washington pursued him across New Jersey, planning to engage him in a battle at Mon'mouth (1778).

Here Lee, who had been exchanged for Prescott, and was again in command, disobeyed orders, and bade his men retreat. Warned by Lafayette, Washington came up just in time to check this movement, and, dashing up to Lee, hotly asked what his disobedience meant. Lee answered: "These men cannot face the British grenadiers." But Washington exclaimed: "They can do it, and they shall!" He was right; the men could, and did, face the enemy bravely. But precious time had been lost, and instead of winning a victory, the Americans only managed to stand their ground.

Molly Pitcher.
During the battle, Molly Pitcher, a gunner's wife, carrying a pail of water to her husband, saw him fall. She immediately rushed forward, took his place, and, loading his

cannon, fired it as quickly and well as he. In reward for filling her husband's place that day, Congress paid her a small pension, and the soldiers, who admired her pluck, ever after called her "Major Molly."

When darkness came on, the fight ceased, and Washington flung himself down to rest. During the night an officer drew softly near, and the general quickly bade him advance and deliver his message, saying: "I lie here to think, and not to sleep." Washington's thoughts were busy, for now he could no longer doubt that Charles Lee was a traitor. Indeed, he foresaw what soon happened—that Lee would be dismissed from the army in disgrace. In fact, Lee, who had tried to harm the American cause, was never allowed to serve his country again, and had to withdraw to Virginia. There he lived a loveless and solitary life, in a house whose only partitions were chalk lines across the floor.

LXXIII. PUTNAM'S ADVENTURES.

On the morrow of the battle of Monmouth, Washington found that Clinton had withdrawn his army so as to avoid a second battle. The British were now well on their way to New York, so Washington could no longer hope to overtake them. To hem them in, however, he stretched a line of American troops all the way from Morristown to West Point.

But Washington had to abandon his plan for seizing New York with the help of the French fleet, because the vessels drew too much water to be able to cross the bar. As the fleet could not reach New York, it made an attempt to seize Newport. Here it was met by British ships; but before a battle could take place, a sudden storm scattered both fleets, and caused so much damage that they had to refit.

When Clinton saw that Washington had drawn a close line about him in New Jersey, he tried to force the American general to break it by attacking the towns in Connecticut. But Washington would not stir, for he knew that General Israel Putnam, in charge of the forces there, was well able to look out for himself. As this Putnam is one of the heroes of the Revolutionary War, it will interest you to hear a few stories about him, which all Americans should know.

We are told that, even as a lad, Putnam was famous for his courage. Once, when a wolf caused great damage in his neighbors' herds, he determined to kill it. But the wolf withdrew into its den, where it could be reached only by crawling along through a narrow passage. As the creature could neither be smoked nor starved out, Putnam offered to go in and kill it. Tying a rope to his foot, he bade his companions pull him out when they felt the rope twitch, or heard a shot. Then he crawled along the passage on his stomach, carefully holding his gun. At the end of a few minutes he came to a place where the passage widened a little, and there, in the darkness, he saw the yellow gleam of the big wolf's eyes! Putnam raised his gun, shot, and was dragged out by his companions in such haste that his clothes were actually torn off his back, and his skin somewhat scraped.

Determined to know whether the old wolf was dead, Putnam, at the end of a few minutes, again crept into the den. When his companions obeyed the twitch of the rope a few minutes later, and drew him out a second time, they thought he was very heavy; but when he got out they found he was dragging by the leg the biggest gray wolf they had ever seen!

Putnam had taken part in the last French and Indian War. The year after the French took and destroyed Fort William Henry, he was with a British army that encamped on the same ground; and when this army advanced to attack Ticonderoga, his company led the way. While they were thus marching through the woods, the French surprised them; and had it not been that Rogers came to their rescue with more men, Putnam and his detachment would have fallen. At another time, we are told, Fort Edward took fire, and the powder magazine was in great danger. But Putnam fought the flames inch by inch, putting them out barely in time to prevent the explosion of the whole store of ammunition.

During this French and Indian War Putnam once volunteered to mount guard at a place where the sentinel was always found dead in the morning. While watching there, he heard a strange noise in the bushes, and saw what he took in the darkness for a wild pig or a bear. He fired at it without a moment's delay, and, on drawing near, found he had killed an Indian, who, covered by a bearskin, and imitating the actions of an animal, had always managed to get near enough to the sentinels to kill them.

Another time, when Putnam and Rogers were sent to recapture some baggage wagons, the latter spent the noon hour in target practice, although warned it was dangerous. The Indians, guided by the sound of firing, fell upon the British unawares, and seizing Putnam bound him to a tree.

For a while Putnam found himself between the fire of his own party and that of the Indians; and when the latter were driven from the battlefield, they took him away with them. After torturing him in many ways, breaking his jaw and cutting open his cheek, the Indians tied him to a tree and began to roast him alive.

The fire was raging around him when a sudden and violent shower put it out. But as soon as the rain was over the savages rekindled it. They would have succeeded in roasting Putnam alive, had not a French officer come up just then, rushed into the fire, cut him loose, and thus saved him from a horrible death.

Burned, gashed, disfigured, and bowed down by weakness, Putnam was taken to Montreal, where the other prisoners were careful not to tell who he was. So the French, thinking him a poor old man who would never have the strength to fight again, gladly exchanged him for one of their captive soldiers.

Putnam then went on fighting again till the war was over. He took an active part in the capture of Montreal in 1760, and in that of Havana two years later.

A British general once showed him a French vessel on Lake Ontario, saying it must be destroyed. Putnam immediately volunteered to destroy it, and rowing out in the dark, he secretly drove wedges behind the rudder. As the vessel could no longer obey its helm, it was soon driven ashore and wrecked.

LXXIV. INDIAN CRUELTY.

The French and Indian War ended, Putnam resumed work on his Connecticut farm. At the time of the Stamp Act trouble he and some of his fellow-citizens visited the house of one of the men who had stamped paper for sale. They told him he must not sell a single sheet of it; and when he objected that he must mind the king, Putnam declared that if he dared disobey them his house would "be level with the dust in five minutes."

Putnam's Ride.

You have already seen how quick Putnam was to respond to the call when the patriots flew to arms. Ever since the beginning of the war he had been equally active. Called upon to meet the British in Connecticut, with but very few men, Putnam nevertheless managed to hamper their movements greatly.

On one occasion he found himself almost surrounded by the British. Calling to his companions to save themselves, he drew off the British soldiers, who hotly pursued him. With the enemy on three sides of him, and a frightfully steep and rocky slope on the other, it seemed quite impossible that Putnam should escape. But he boldly drove his spurs into his steed, rode safely down the stone steps at Horse'neck, and as none of the British dared follow him, he thus managed to get away.

Hearing that the British were burning farmhouses and villages in Connecticut, Washington fancied it might be a good plan to strike a blow which would frighten them and make them come back. He therefore planned to storm Stony Point, a place on the Hudson, where the British were building a new fort.

Sending for Anthony Wayne, an officer who was so brave and daring that his men generally called him "Mad Anthony," Washington told him what he wanted. The young man, devoted to Washington, promptly cried: "I'll storm hell, general, if you will only plan it!" The patriotic young soldier's answer was so well meant that Washington, who never swore himself, and generally reproved his men when they did so, merely smiled on this occasion, and quietly said: "Hadn't we better try Stony Point first?"

The Americans, with guns unloaded and bayonets fixed, drew near the fort unseen, led by an old negro who often went in and out of the British camp to sell strawberries. He walked up to the sentinel, and whispered: "The fort is ours." As this was the password, the soldier began to chat with him, and thus did not notice the Americans creeping up behind him until they seized and gagged him.

The Capture of Stony Point.

The patriots thus got halfway up the hill before the alarm was given and firing began. Although one of the first shots wounded Mad Anthony, he bade his men carry him, and, cheering his soldiers on, led the way into the fort. Taken by surprise, the British lost many men and their new fort, and at two o'clock in the morning Wayne wrote to Washington: "The fort and garrison, with Colonel Johnson, are ours. Our officers and men behaved like men who are determined to be free." This charge at Stony Point (1779) is considered one of the most brilliant deeds of the Revolutionary War, and the place where it occurred is often visited.

When war first broke out the British hired many Indians to fight for them. While the two main armies were busy in New Jersey, southern New York, and Connecticut, people living in northern New York, and all along the western frontier, were in constant danger. Led by a man named Butler, some Tories—friends of the king—and many Indians suddenly appeared in the Wy-o'ming Valley, in Pennsylvania. Here they cruelly murdered men, women, and children. We are even told that a cruel soldier once ran his bayonet through a tiny baby, and tossed it out of its cradle, saying it was a rebel also!

Not satisfied with one raid of this kind, the Indians soon made a second one at Cherry Valley, in New York. These massacres roused the Americans' anger, not only against the Indians, but also against the British for hiring the help of such cruel allies. Still, it was only the king and some of his ministers who were to blame for this, for most Englishmen felt like Burke. When the order had been given to make use of the Indians, but forbidding them to be cruel, Burke made a speech in the House of Commons, saying: "Suppose there was a riot on Tower Hill. What would the keeper of his Majesty's lions do? Would he not fling open the dens of the wild beasts, and then address them thus: 'My gentle lions, my humane bears, my tender-hearted hyenas, go forth! But I exhort you, as you are Christians and members of civilized society, to take care not to hurt any man, woman, or child!'"

To punish the Indians for the massacres at Wyoming Valley and Cherry Valley, General Sul´li-van now marched into the Indian territory, where he burned more than forty villages. He also killed so many warriors that the Indians in that part of the country never again dared rise up against the Americans.

The Indian war not only raged in the northeast, but extended even into what is now Ken-tuck´y. Although there were but very few settlers there then, many of these were slain. To put an end to Indian raids, General George Rogers Clark of Virginia marched northward, hoping to conquer all the land between the Ohio, the Lakes, and the Mississippi.

Clark's March.

Although his army was small, it was composed of brave men, used to the woods and to the Indian way of fighting. They followed him boldly through the wilderness, fording rivers and streams. We are told that they once came to water so deep that their little drummer boy, seeing it would rise above his head, used his drum as a raft, begging the tallest soldier to steer him safely across.

Marching thus from point to point, Clark's forces took all the forts in the Illinois country; but as he had few men, he could not send fair-sized garrisons to all. Some time after Vin-cennes´ submitted, a large British force appeared to capture it, and loudly commanded the American officer there to surrender. After some parley, this man consented to do so, provided he and his garrison were allowed to march out with all the honors of war.

The British officer granted this request; but imagine his surprise and anger when he saw the officer march out, followed by only one man! These two composed the whole garrison, and could boast that they had held the fort of Vincennes against a force of eight hundred men. When Clark heard what had happened, he marched over with a large force and recaptured the fort.

LXXV. BOONE IN KENTUCKY.

As you have heard, the land south of the Ohio suffered much from Indian raids. This part of the country had already been the scene of so many Indian battles that it well deserved the name of Kentucky, or the "dark and bloody ground." Six years before the Revolutionary War began, Daniel Boone, a hardy pioneer, first crossed the Alleghany Mountains and came into this beautiful region. Seeing the tall forest trees and plentiful game, he thought it would be a good place to live in.

After wandering about it for months, and escaping from the hands of some Indians who had taken him captive, Boone made up his mind to settle there. He therefore went back to North Carolina for his wife and daughter, and, with his brother and several other pioneers, returned to Kentucky where he formed a settlement called Boones´bor-o (1775). Like all pioneer villages, this was merely a collection of a few log huts, surrounded by a tall palisade to serve as a rampart against Indian attacks.

Boone's daughter and two younger girls, little suspecting danger, once went out in a canoe to pick flowers along the banks of a stream. Suddenly several Indians sprang out of a thicket, seized them, and bore them off into the woods. While the younger girls cried helplessly, Boone's daughter, seeing it was of no use to struggle, quietly followed her captor. But she took care to leave the print of her shoe here and there where the soil was damp, to break twigs of bushes, and to fasten shreds of her dress to the briers along the way, so that her tracks could be followed.

As soon as the girls' capture was discovered, Boone and six other men set out in pursuit. Thanks to the girl's clever way of marking her passage, they soon came to where the savages were camping in the woods. Creeping up stealthily, the white men noiselessly got between the children and the Indians, for they knew the latter would kill and scalp their captives at the first alarm. The Indians, suddenly finding themselves in danger, hastily fled, leaving captives and weapons behind them.

In the third year of the Revolutionary War, some Indians, hired by the British to make war along the frontier, came to attack Boonesboro. But the place was so gallantly defended by the settlers that they could not get in. They vainly directed a steady fire against the palisades for some time, and then withdrew to a short distance to rest.

The settlers, who had very little powder within the palisade, were anxious to secure a keg full of powder that was standing in a hut near by. Still, they knew that if a man ventured out, the Indians would probably kill him, and they did not feel that they could spare a single one. A brave girl, Elizabeth Zane, therefore insisted upon going, for she said they could easily get along without her, although they needed all the men.

Elizabeth Zane brings Powder.

At her request, the gate was opened, and she sped like an arrow to the house where the powder had been left. The Indians, astonished at the sight of a woman running out of the fort, stood perfectly still. In a few seconds they saw her rush back, her apron full of powder. Now they understood what it all meant; but it was too late to stop the brave girl, who had reached the fort in safety. The powder thus secured saved the settlement; for the Indians, after losing many men, gave up the siege and went home.

In 1778, while out hunting, Boone was captured by Indians, who carried him off to Detroit. They were about to kill him when an old squaw claimed him to take the place of her son who had been slain. The Indians consented, and Boone was adopted by the squaw, who pulled out all his hair, except a scalp lock, which she dressed with feathers in fine Indian style.

Boone now made believe to be quite satisfied to stay with the Indians; so they took him out hunting every day, giving him only a certain amount of powder and bullets. Boone was such a good marksman that he soon found he could kill his game with half a bullet and less powder. He therefore secretly cut his bullets in two, and although he brought back a bird, rabbit, or deer for every charge the savages gave him, he really saved half his ammunition without their suspecting it.

When he had thus collected enough powder and bullets, Boone stole a piece of dried meat and some parched corn, and went out hunting, as usual. But as soon as he got out of sight he began running as hard as he could. As he ran he hid his traces, so the Indians could not follow him. Thus he darted along fallen trees, jumped from stone to stone, ran up and down shallow streams, and once, at least, grasped a trailing grapevine, and, swinging hard, landed on his feet a long distance ahead.

The Indians, finding out his escape, soon started to follow him; but while they were hunting around for his broken tracks, he ran on, pausing to rest only when his strength gave out. Boone thus reached the Ohio, where he had the good luck to find a leaky canoe, in which he paddled across the stream.

Then, for the first time, he used one of the bullets he had saved to kill a turkey, which he roasted over the first fire he had dared to light since his escape. Tramping thus all the way from the Indian camp to Boonesboro, Boone found his home deserted. At first he thought all his family had been killed; but he soon heard they had merely gone back to their old home, thinking he was dead.

Boone's Grapevine.

As he knew the Indians would soon come to attack Boonesboro, Boone collected about fifty-five men, who helped him repair the palisade. They were scarcely through their work when more than four hundred Indians appeared, led by a French officer serving in the British army. When they bade Boone surrender, he answered: "We are determined to defend our fort while a man of us lives."

Although the Indians tried to break into the fort, they were driven back, and their bullets had no effect on the heavy logs of the palisade. Next they made an attempt to set fire to the fort, but the flames were quickly quenched; and when they began to tunnel a way into the place, they were forced to give it up.

Weary of vain attempts, the Indians finally withdrew; and when they had gone, Boone and his companions picked up a hundred and twenty-five pounds of bullets, which had fallen harmlessly along the palisade. Later on, Boone brought his family back to Kentucky; but the Indians continued to make trouble during the next ten years. Still, when those dark days were all over, so many settlers came into Kentucky that Boone declared the place was too crowded for him, and said he needed more elbow-room.

He therefore removed first to a place near the Great Ka-na´wha, and then to Missouri, which at that time belonged to Spain. Here he lived long enough to see many settlers cross the Mississippi. He was again saying that he felt crowded, and talking of moving still farther west, when he died, at the age of eighty-five, still hale and hearty, and a famous hunter and pioneer.

LXXVI. FAMOUS SEA FIGHTS.

While American patriots were busy fighting the British on land, others, equally brave, were fighting them at sea. As soon as the war began, Congress gave seamen letters of marque, which were permissions to attack and seize any British vessel they met.

The bravest and best known of all the American seamen of this time was John Paul Jones. Although born in Scotland, he adopted this country for his own, and, when the War of Independence began, offered his services to Congress. He proved such an able seaman that in 1777 he was sent to France on an important errand. Although the French did not give him a large ship, as he had hoped, he boldly cruised around in a little American vessel called the *Ranger*, on which he hoisted the first American flag ever seen and saluted at sea.

Paul Jones sailed boldly along, capturing and sinking English vessels, and even running into the port of White-ha´ven, where he tried to burn all the shipping. Then, as his boat was no longer good enough to continue fighting, he went back to France, in quest of a long-promised new ship. But after five months' weary delay, he was still ashore and waiting.

One day he read in "Poor Richard's Almanac": "If you would have your business done, go; if not, send." This saying seemed so true that he immediately set out for Paris. There he managed to talk to the French minister, who again promised him a fine ship. But when the young seaman saw this craft, five days later, he was sorely disappointed, for it was both old and clumsy.

Still, any kind of a ship was better than no ship at all; so Paul Jones named it *Bonhomme Richard* (bŏ-nŏm´ re-shar´), a French translation of "Poor Richard." Then he set sail in it, accompanied by a few smaller vessels, and coasted along the North Sea. There Jones ran near the shore, where his visits were so dreaded that, we are told, an old Scotch minister at Kirk-cal´dy once prayed: "Now, dear Lord, don't you think it a shame for you to send this vile pirate to rob our folk of Kirkcaldy? You know that they are poor enough already, and have nothing to spare."

Still, Paul Jones was not so vile a pirate as the old minister supposed, for whenever he landed for provisions, he paid the poor people for the food and cattle he took. We are also told that, his men having once robbed a castle of its silver plate, Jones sent it all back, eight years later, with a polite note.

But while Jones did not wish to harm the poor, he did want to damage the British navy as much as he could. He therefore cruised about until he met the *Se-rā´pis*, a British man-of-war, off Flam´-bor-ough Head(1779). Here was waged one of the fiercest naval battles ever fought. Although Jones's ship was afire from the very beginning, his guns all disabled, the vessel shot away between decks and slowly sinking, he boldly lashed it fast to the *Serapis*. While doing so he heard one of his men swear, and turning to him, quietly said: "Don't swear, sir; in another moment we may all be in eternity."

The Bonhomme Richard and the Serapis.

By this time the smoke was so thick that the British captain could not see whether the American flag had been hauled down. He therefore shouted: "Have you struck your colors?" But Jones coolly answered: "I have not yet begun to fight." Such was Jones's pluck that the British commander finally yielded; but when he gave up his sword to Paul Jones, he haughtily said: "It is with great reluctance that I surrender my sword to a man who fights with a halter round his neck."

Paul Jones gave him back the weapon, politely saying: "Captain Pearson, you have fought like a hero, and I have no doubt that your sovereign will reward you for it in the most ample manner." These words came true, for after Captain Pearson had been duly exchanged, George III. called him to court and made him a knight.

As the *Bonhomme Richard* was sinking, Jones transferred his men and prisoners to the *Serapis*. Then he sadly watched his own ship settle down and vanish beneath the waves. The *Serapis* was next taken to France, where it was discovered that Captain Landais (lahN-dā´), the French commander of one of the smaller vessels in Jones's fleet, was insane. Paul Jones and his men had known this for some time, because Landais had disobeyed orders several times, and when the *Bonhomme Richard* was fighting against the *Serapis*, he had even used his cannon against it instead of attacking the enemy.

The news of Paul Jones's victory caused great rejoicings both in America and in France, and when the young captain returned to the latter country, he was invited to court with Franklin. King Louis XVI. heard Jones's account of the fight, and told him that his enemy, Captain Pearson had just been knighted, and had received a new ship. Paul Jones then gayly answered: "Well, he deserved the honor, and if I meet him in his new ship I'll make a lord of him."

This answer greatly amused the king; but at the same time it showed that Paul Jones, hero as he was, had one great fault—that of boasting. When he came back to America, Congress honored him; but as the young sailor did not think his services were well enough appreciated in America, he left our country soon after the war was ended, and went to serve Russia.

Paul Jones was not the only hero on the seas at this time, for we are told the American privateers captured five hundred British vessels in three years, secured much booty, and did great harm to the shipping in several English ports.

LXXVII. THE "SWAMP FOX."

The British had failed not only in their first attempt, against Boston, but also in their second,—to seize the Hudson valley and thus separate the southern colonies from New England. But as they were not yet ready to give up the struggle, they decided to try a third plan. That was to begin a new campaign in the far south, and march up the Atlantic coast, leaving nothing but conquered people behind them.

In 1778, therefore, they began their operations by besieging and taking Savannah. Soon after, they became masters of Au-gus´ta and of nearly all Georgia. These successes delighted them, for, with one province won, they fancied they would soon be masters of all the rest. Still, before they could do much more, the French fleet under D'Estaing (des-taN´), and an American army under Lincoln, came to recover Savannah. While the French were bombarding that city from their ships, the Americans, led by Pulaski, tried to storm it (1779).

But in spite of a most gallant charge, the patriots were driven back with great loss. Among the dead was Sergeant Jasper, still holding the flag given him at Fort Moultrie, and Count Pulaski, the generous Pole who had joined the army and served under Washington in the battle of the Brandywine. Both of these men were so brave that their names will never be forgotten, and in Savannah fine monuments have been erected in their honor.

Pulaski's Monument in Savannah.

The first attempt to take Savannah having failed, the French admiral refused to lend any more aid to the Americans in the South. So Lincoln, after defending Charleston alone for forty days, was forced to surrender. The British, coming to the city, exacted such hard conditions from him that they roused the indignation of all true Americans. But when the British minister heard that the city was taken, he proudly cried: "We look on America as at our feet!"

The British now overran the state, behaving most cruelly everywhere. An officer named Tarle´ton not only burned houses, and beat women and children, but when some Americans asked for quarter,—that is, vowed not to fight any more if he would spare their lives,—he broke his promise and had them all killed. Because he did not keep his word, the expression "Tarleton's quarter" was used in the South as a term for immediate death.

Although by Lincoln's surrender one American army was lost, the patriots were not ready to give up yet, and as soon as another force was raised, Gates was sent southward to command it. He was so proud of his victory at Saratoga that he started out full of confidence. When he stopped, on his way, to visit Lee, the latter, hearing him boast, quietly remarked: "Take care your northern laurels do not turn to southern willows."

Unfortunately, however, Gates paid no heed to this warning. Thinking he would soon force Cornwallis to surrender, he was very imprudent, and when he met the British at Cam´den, a few months later (1780), he suffered a defeat instead of winning a victory. We are told that when he saw the day was lost, Gates turned and fled, never daring to stop until he had put about eighty miles between himself and his foes. The German officer De Kalb, who had so generously come to help the Americans, fought in this battle with great courage, and died from the eleven wounds he received there. He is buried at Camden, where a monument marks his resting place. This was the worst battle for the Americans during the whole war, and it was speedily followed by the loss of nearly all South Carolina. The only people who still had courage to fight were a few patriots led by such heroes as Mār´i-on, Sumter, and Pickens.

The first of these three men was so upright, brave, and gentlemanly that he has often been compared to a brave French knight, and is therefore known as the "Bay´ard of the South." Marion and his men had retreats in the woods and swamps, whence they made sudden raids upon the British. It seems that the latter, wishing to exchange prisoners, once sent an officer into one of these hiding places under a flag of truce. As Marion did not wish the British to learn the way to his retreat, this officer was blindfolded and led a long distance. When his bandage was removed, he was surprised to find himself, not in a fort or house, as he had expected, but in a lonely spot in the woods. Marion stepped forward, politely offered him a seat on a log, and, when business was over, cordially invited him to share his dinner.

The officer was just wondering where his dining room could be, when one of the ragged soldiers appeared, carrying a piece of bark on which smoked some sweet potatoes, roasted in the camp fire. Marion helped his guest to a potato on a chip, and began to eat one himself with a relish. Of course the British officer immediately followed his example; but he soon asked whether the American officers often dined so simply. Marion, the "Swamp Fox," answered, "Yes;" and then gayly added, "but we are fortunate on this occasion, having company to entertain, to have more than our usual allowance."

Marion's Dinner.

The officer, hearing this, suggested that the Americans probably gave their soldiers big pay to make up for such poor fare and uncomfortable quarters. But Marion truthfully answered that he received no salary at all. The astonished officer then asked why he served such a mean country at all; and the brave young Southerner, looking him full in the face, proudly remarked that a man was always ready to do anything for the lady he loved, and that the name of his sweetheart was Liberty.

The British officer could not but admire such a man and such an answer. On returning to camp, we are told, he left the service, saying he would have no share in depriving such brave men as Marion of the rights due them.

LXXVIII. THE POOR SOLDIERS.

In the meantime things were going very badly in the North. The winter spent at Valley Forge had, indeed, been hard to bear, but that which Washington spent at Morristown was in some respects even worse. Congress, in those days, had no power to tax the people to raise money, the states were in many cases too poor to supply much, and it was very difficult to borrow funds abroad, because it was quite evident that if the Americans were beaten their debts would never be paid.

Already in 1777 Congress began to issue paper money. Of course it had no real value of its own, like gold or silver, but was merely a promise that Congress would some day give the bearer the amount it called for in real money. As everybody knew that Congress did not have, and therefore could not give, gold or silver in exchange for these "continental bills," no one liked to take them in payment for food or clothing.

To make matters worse, the British printed ever so many bills just like those issued by Congress, and paper money soon became so nearly worthless as to give rise to the expression still used, "Not worth a continental." By this time there was two hundred millions' worth of this money in circulation, and people gave one hundred and fifty dollars in bills for a bushel of corn, and several thousand for a suit of clothes, when they had no silver or gold.

Many times during the Revolutionary War the soldiers, knowing their families were starving, clamored loudly for their money. As it was not paid to them, some of them rebelled, and it took all their love for Washington—the only person whom they really trusted—to hold the army together. Still, these soldiers were faithful to their country; for when British spies once came among them, offering gold if they would only desert, they nobly gave these spies up to their officers, saying that, while they wanted their dues, they were not traitors.

The British not only tried to win over the men, but also attempted to bribe American officers and statesmen. But they failed in this, too; and when they approached Joseph Reed, he proudly said: "I am not worth purchasing; but such as I am, the King of Great Britain is not rich enough to buy me."

Washington always supplied the needs of his men as far as he could; but as he had been away from Mount Vernon several years now, his fortune was much smaller than it had been, and as time went on he had less and less ready money. In despair at his men's sufferings, he wrote again and again to Congress. Finally he warned Robert Morris, who had charge of money matters, that it would be impossible to keep the army together if food, money, and clothing were not forthcoming right away.

This appeal proved successful. Morris not only gave all the money he had, but, going from door to door, begged from all his friends for the safety of the country. The Philadelphians nobly answered his appeal, and on New Year's Day Washington could gladden the soldiers' hearts by giving them food and money. Shortly after, the Philadelphia ladies, wishing to help also, sent him twenty-two thousand shirts, which they had made for the almost naked soldiers, who were glad to get into warm and whole garments.

LXXIX. THE SPY.

You may remember that Benedict Arnold marched gallantly through the Maine woods to attack Quebec, and was wounded there in the beginning of the war. After his recovery he showed his courage in many ways. For instance, he was once surrounded by Tories, who killed his horse. While Arnold was trying to release his foot from the stirrup, one of his foes rushed toward him, crying, "Surrender!" "Not yet," answered Arnold, and, drawing his pistol, he shot the Tory, jumped up, and ran into the woods near by. There, finding another horse, he quickly mounted, and came back to take part in the fight once more.

You remember, too, how he won the victory of Stillwater, with Morgan and Schuyler, while Gates was lingering idly in his tent. On this occasion, however, Arnold was again badly wounded. As he lay upon the ground, helpless, one of the enemy, who had fought with great valor and had fallen only a moment before him, slowly raised himself, and, in spite of a bad wound, tried to get at Arnold to kill him. Just then a friend of Arnold's came up, and was about to slay the soldier, when Arnold stopped him by crying: "For God's sake, don't hurt him; he is a fine fellow!"

Although Arnold could thus show himself both brave and forgiving, he had one great fault, his vanity. While recovering from his wound, in Philadelphia, he got into bad company, ran into debt, and behaved in such a way that Congress bade Washington reprove him publicly for his conduct. Washington did so as gently as he could, and some time later, when Arnold asked him for the command at West Point, he gladly granted this request; for he knew that Arnold was brave, and thought he had been treated rather unfairly. But no sooner had Arnold secured this important place than, forgetting his duty to his country and his honor as a man, he determined to avenge his wrongs by giving up the fort to the British (1780). He therefore began a secret correspondence with General Clinton, and finally arranged to meet a British officer, so as to settle the particulars of the affair with him.

True to the appointment, Major John André came up the Hudson in an English vessel, the *Vulture*. Landing at night, he met Arnold as agreed; but their talk lasted until morning, and the ship, being then discovered by the Americans, was fired upon. It therefore dropped down the river. Seeing that he could not join it without running too great a risk of discovery, André now got a pass from Arnold. He then crossed the Hudson, and set out for New York on horseback, reaching Tăr´ry-town in safety, although travelers were then often stopped by parties of "Skinners" or "Cowboys," as marauding British and American troops were generally called. André was just beginning to think that all danger of capture was over, when three men suddenly sprang out of the bushes, seized his horse, and forced him to dismount.

Although André offered his horse, his watch, and a large sum of money to these three men if they would only let him go, they held him fast and began searching him. At first they found nothing suspicious; but in his boots they finally discovered plans of the fort at West Point, and other important papers.

André and his Captors.

Sure that they held a spy, Paulding, Williams, and Van Wart now sent word to Arnold to look out, for they had caught a spy, and then they took André to White Plains. Arnold was at breakfast when the notice of André's capture reached him. Rising from the table, he hurriedly explained matters to his fainting wife, kissed his child good-by, and, mounting his horse, galloped wildly off to the river. There he found his boat, as usual, and was rowed off to the *Vulture*. The British, who had watched his approach, received him in grim silence; for while they would have been glad to take advantage of his baseness, they all despised him as a traitor.

Washington, then on his way to West Point, received the news of André's arrest too late to seize Arnold, although he tried very hard to do so. Still, he did not forget that Arnold's wife was innocent. Pitying her evident suffering, he soon sent her word that her husband had escaped, and said that she would be allowed to join him in New York.

The news of Arnold's treachery, which wrung tears from Washington, and made him exclaim, "Whom can we trust now?" filled the whole country with dismay. People were horror-struck; but while all hated Arnold, many were almost as excited over the capture and probable fate of André. An artist, writer, and soldier, this young man had many admirers; but as he had played the part of a spy, and had been captured in disguise within the American lines, most people thought he deserved to be hanged.

Still, it was felt that Arnold, the traitor, was the one who merited that death most, so when the British protested that André should not be hanged, the Americans offered to exchange him for Arnold, thinking that if they could only make an example of the real culprit it would prevent similar cases in the future.

But, much as the British despised Arnold, they could not, of course, give him up. André's trial, therefore, went on, and the jury condemned him to death as a spy. Instead of treating him as the British had treated Hale, however, the Americans allowed him to write to his friends and prepare for death. When he was ready, André paid the penalty of his wrongdoing by being hanged. Still, people have always felt sorry for him, and the British, who would have gained greatly by his spying, declared that he had fallen a martyr. They therefore gave him a place in Westminster Abbey, where many of their greatest men are buried. Besides, two monuments have been erected for him in our country, at Tarrytown and Tap´pan, thus marking the places where he was captured and hanged.

But, although André was hanged, his sufferings were slight and merciful compared with those of Arnold. This was just; for, while the former had tried to serve his country, the latter had betrayed his trust, and it was natural that his conscience should trouble him night and day. Although the British, as they had promised, gave him a large sum of money and a place in their army, none of their officers ever treated him as a friend.

We are told that Washington, still anxious to secure and punish Arnold for the country's sake, made a plan to seize him shortly after his escape. An officer named Campe deserted the American army, by Washington's orders, and—narrowly escaping recapture by his comrades, who were not in the secret—swam out to a British vessel anchored in New York Bay. The enemy, having breathlessly watched his escape from his pursuers, welcomed him warmly, and, without asking any questions, allowed him to enlist in Arnold's new regiment.

Campe intended, with the help of two other patriots, to seize and gag Arnold when he was walking alone in his garden, as he did every night. Thence they meant to convey him to a boat, row him secretly across the river, and hand him over to one of Washington's most devoted officers, Henry Lee, who was called "Light-Horse Harry," to distinguish him from the Lee who disgraced himself at Monmouth.

Unfortunately, on the very night when Campe's plan was to have been carried out, Arnold took his regiment on board a vessel in the bay, and sailed south to fight for the British in Virginia. There poor Campe had to wait for months before he got a chance to desert Arnold and rejoin his countrymen. Until then all his fellow-soldiers had believed him a real deserter; but after welcoming him cordially, Washington and Lee publicly told the others how nobly Campe had tried to serve his country, and how nearly he had secured the traitor.

While fighting in the South, we are told, Arnold once asked one of his prisoners, "What do you suppose my fate would be if my misguided countrymen were to take me prisoner?" The man, who was a good American, promptly answered: "They would cut off the leg that was wounded at Quebec and Saratoga, and bury it with the honors of war; but the rest of you they would hang on a gibbet."

LXXX. A TRAITOR'S DEATH.

Before continuing the story of the Revolutionary War, it is well to finish this painful story of a traitor. After fighting against his country in Virginia, and burning many houses and villages there, Arnold was sent into Connecticut, where he set fire to New London, watching the flames from the church tower. But soon after this Arnold went to London, where he spent most of the rest of his life, with few friends.

We are told that no one respected him there, and once, when he went into Parliament to hear the speeches, a member pointed right at him, saying: "Mr. Speaker, I will not speak while that man is in the house." Another time Arnold was introduced to a British officer who had fought against him at Saratoga. But, while this man had then admired him for his courage, and would have been proud to know him, he now refused to shake hands with him, curtly saying that he could not endure traitors.

A gentleman who did not know Arnold's story once asked him for letters of introduction to his friends, saying he was about to sail for America. But the traitor sadly answered: "I was born in America; I lived there to the prime of my life; but, alas! I can call no man in America my friend." In fact, even his children were so ashamed of what he had done that two of his sons changed their name as soon as they grew up.

After living thus twenty years, bereft of his own as well as public respect, Arnold on his deathbed begged for the epaulets and sword-knot which Washington had once given him, and cried: "Let me die in my old American uniform, in which I fought my battles. God forgive me for ever having put on any other!"

Arnold was buried in England. While his victories are honored in America, his treachery has made his name so disliked that it is always coupled with the words "the traitor." The battles of Saratoga, where he, Schuyler, and Morgan really won the victories attributed to Gates, are kept in mind by history and by the beautiful monument at Saratoga. There you can see four niches. Three are occupied by statues of Gates, Schuyler, and Morgan; but the fourth—which was to contain a statue of Arnold—must always remain empty!

The sadness which filled all patriot hearts in the country at the news of Arnold's treason was, however, soon made more bearable by the welcome tidings of a victory in the South—the battle of Kings Mountain (1780).

Battle of Kings Mountain.

More than a thousand of the British troops took up their position on the top of this mountain, and their leader then cried: "Well, boys, here is a place from which all the rebels outside of hell cannot drive us!" Still, a smaller number of patriots climbed up by three different paths, and, hiding behind rocks and trees, killed many of the British, and took the rest prisoners.

General Greene, taking command of the American forces in the South after Gates's defeat at Camden, found himself at the head of a ragged and almost famished army. But stout hearts beat beneath tattered garments, and the forces under Morgan soon after won a great victory at Cowpens (1781).

The cruel Tarleton was in command on this occasion, and during the battle he was wounded by Colonel William Washington, a distant relative of the general in chief. In speaking of the battle afterwards, Tarleton scornfully remarked to an American lady that Colonel Washington was so ignorant a man that he could not even write his own name. As people who could not write in those days were in the habit of making a rough mark instead of signing their names, the lady archly said, pointing to his wound: "Ah, colonel, you bear evidence that he can at least make his mark!" When Tarleton later added that he wondered what Colonel Washington looked like, the same lady slyly said: "Had you only looked behind you at Cowpens, you might have had that pleasure."

LXXXI. TWO UNSELFISH WOMEN.

When the battle of Cowpens was over, and the few remnants of Tarleton's force had fled to join Cornwallis, the latter marched forward, hoping to catch up with Morgan's army and crush it with his superior force before it could join Greene's forces. Both armies were therefore anxious to reach the ford over the Ca-taw´ba first, and tramped ahead as fast as possible, stopping to rest only when the men were completely exhausted. But, in spite of the great odds against him, Morgan finally managed to give Cornwallis the slip, and, crossing at the ford, was soon joined by Greene. The two generals continued the retreat, cleverly tempting Cornwallis to follow, until finally the whole American army was safe beyond the Dan River in Virginia.

We are told that it was during this race for the Dan that Greene once stopped at the house of a patriot Southern lady, Mrs. Steele. She quickly supplied him with warm garments and food, and hearing him say he could not pay her because he was penniless, she brought him all her savings, which she forced him to accept and use for the sake of his country.

It seems also that in the course of this campaign the Americans laid siege to a house which served as a fort for British soldiers. Although Light-Horse Harry Lee was very anxious to secure these men, he soon found that he could not drive them out of the house. He therefore asked Mrs. Motte, owner of the place, whether she would allow him to set fire to it, to force the British out.

She not only consented to this,—although the house was all she had,—but brought Lee an Indian bow and arrows, so that he could shoot bits of flaming wood upon the shingled roof. The house was thus soon in flames, and the British, seeing they would be roasted alive if they staid in it, and shot if they tried to escape, promptly surrendered. Then the fire was put out, and as it had not yet gained much headway, Mrs. Motte did not, after all, lose the house which she had been willing to sacrifice for the sake of her country.

As was the case all through the Southern campaign, the British were very cruel; still, a few patriots managed to escape from their clutches. For example, one of Tarleton's men once ordered a prisoner to give him the silver buckles he wore. The man proudly bade the Englishman take them if he wanted them. Knowing that he would be slain if he did not escape, the American killed the man kneeling before him, and, jumping on a riderless horse, dashed away. Before any of the four hundred men around there thought of pursuing him, he was out of reach.

As soon as his men had rested a little from their fatigues, Greene again led them against the British, whom he met at Guil'ford Courthouse in North Carolina. Here, although the Americans behaved with great valor, the British won the victory. But it was at the cost of so many lives that when Fox, a British statesman, heard of it, he sadly exclaimed: "Another such victory would ruin us!"

The site of the old Revolutionary battlefield at Guilford Courthouse is now a beautiful park. Here are many interesting statues, and in the museum, among other curiosities, you can see British and American flags peacefully crossed, showing that after the war was over the two parties generously forgot the past and were ready to meet as friends.

After the battle of Guilford Courthouse, Cornwallis retreated to the coast, and Greene turned his attention to the British forces farther south, with which he fought the battles of Hobkirk Hill and Eu'taw Springs. In the latter engagement, Marion, surrounded by the foe, encouraged his brave men by saying: "Hold up your heads, boys! Three fires, three cheers, and a charge, and you are free!" During the same engagement one of Lee's men found himself alone and without arms in the midst of the enemy. With great presence of mind, he seized an officer, wrenched his sword out of his hand, and, using him as a shield, fought his way back to his friends.

Though Greene was often defeated and never won a great victory, the British loudly complained that he never knew when he was beaten. But while Greene modestly described his own doings as, "We fight, get beat, rise and fight again," he and his two thousand men were little by little driving the British out of South Carolina. Indeed, by their brave efforts the Americans finally recovered both South Carolina and Georgia, with the exception of the cities of Charleston and Savannah.

LXXXII. THE SURRENDER OF CORNWALLIS.

Retreating from the Carolinas, Cornwallis marched into Virginia to take the place of Arnold, whom the British had been watching closely, lest he should betray them, too. Clinton now bade Cornwallis keep near the coast, so that he could embark quickly and come to the rescue of New York, in case Washington should suddenly attack it.

The fact was, though, that Washington had no intention of doing anything of the sort. On the contrary, he had laid his plans to catch Cornwallis in Virginia, where he had sent Lafayette some time before. As he did not wish Clinton to suspect this plan, Washington wrote letters saying he meant to take New York, and cleverly contrived that they should accidentally fall into British hands. After reading them, Clinton felt so sure he knew all about the American plans that he did not stir.

There was no telegraph in those days, and it was a great surprise to Cornwallis when the French fleet, under De Grasse (grahss) suddenly appeared in Chesapeake Bay. Thus, even before Clinton suspected the Americans' intentions, Cornwallis was hemmed in at Yorktown between Lafayette's troops and De Grasse's fleet, and Washington was rapidly marching southward to help them.

Hoping to check Washington's advance, or even force him to come back, Clinton now sent Arnold into Connecticut, where, as we have seen, he burned New London. This base deed so angered a lady whose guest he had once been, that she tried to shoot him, we are told, and would have done so, had not her gun missed fire.

Arnold, and the British officers with him, proved very cruel all through this campaign; and when one of them seized Fort Griswold, near New London, he haughtily demanded,

"Who commands here?" "I did," courteously answered the American officer, coming forward to surrender his sword, "but you do now." The British officer took the weapon, ran it through its owner, and coolly bade his men kill all the garrison in the same way.

Although the news of pillage, burning, and murder was carried to Washington as quickly as possible, he did not—as Clinton perhaps expected—turn around to defend Connecticut, but kept steadily on. As he marched by, all good Americans wildly cheered him, crying: "Long live Washington! He is going to catch Cornwallis in his mouse trap!" Indeed, such was the faith people had in him that an old patriot, coming into the room where he was dining, raised his arms to heaven and solemnly cried, like Simeon in the Bible: "Lord, now lettest thou thy servant depart in peace, for mine eyes have seen thy salvation."

On his way to Yorktown, Washington paid a flying visit to his home at Mount Vernon, which he had not seen since he left it to attend the Continental Congress six years before. There he learned that it would have been burned to the ground, had not his steward bribed some British soldiers to let it stand. When Washington heard this, he gravely said that he would rather lose all he had, than save it by making friends with his country's foes.

Reaching Yorktown,—where Cornwallis had once boasted that he would soon capture "that boy," as he scornfully termed Lafayette,—Washington found all his orders so well carried out that the bombarding of the city could begin without further delay. The French fleet and American army worked together to such good purpose that before long it became plain that Cornwallis would have to yield. During this siege a gentleman carefully pointed out his own house, advising Washington to batter it down first with his cannon; for he thought that Cornwallis must have selected it for his headquarters, because it was the best in town.

Washington, who was never wounded in any battle, stood on a height directing the movements of his troops. He was in such an exposed place that some of his aids, hoping to make him change his position, ventured to remark that they were in great danger. "If you think so," answered Washington, quietly, "you are at liberty to step back." But as he did not move, the others bravely stood their ground.

A moment later a ball struck a cannon only a few feet off, and General Knox impulsively cried, "My dear general, we can't spare you yet!" and tried to drag him away. But Washington carelessly remarked, "It's a spent ball," and stood there like a rock until he saw the redoubt taken. Then he joyfully exclaimed: "The work is done, and well done!"

Washington was right; the work was done, and the patriots' troubles nearly over. Cornwallis, finding himself unable to escape or receive help, was forced to surrender on the 19th of October, 1781. But his pride was so hurt at having to give up his sword, that he pretended illness, and sent one of his officers to carry it to Washington. The latter, remembering how the British had tried to shame General Lincoln at the surrender of Charleston, therefore bade the British officer deliver it to Lincoln.

The next day, when the British troops marched out of Yorktown between the French and American armies, their bands dolefully played: "The World Turned Upside Down." Washington, ever considerate of people's feelings, had given strict orders that his soldiers should not jeer at the enemy, or make any unkind remarks. This order was obeyed, but Lafayette, seeing that the British—who had made such unmerciful fun of him—did not even look up, suddenly bade his band strike up "Yankee Doodle." At this hated sound the British all started, and Lafayette had the boyish satisfaction of knowing that they had seen him heading part of the forces which had conquered them.

The Surrender of Cornwallis.

LXXXIII. THE BRITISH FLAG HAULED DOWN.

The news of the surrender of Cornwallis filled all American hearts with joy; for our people knew, as well as the British, that the war was now ended. The tidings reached Philadelphia at night, while the watchman, making his rounds as usual, was passing up and down the streets. To the customary announcement of the time, and the cry, "All's well," he therefore added, "and Cornwallis is taken!"

The joy of this event proved fatal to the old doorkeeper of Congress, while on all sides bells were rung and loud cheers were heard. On the next day the members of Congress marched in a body to church, to return thanks for the "victory of a great and good man in a great and good cause." But when the news reached England it caused great dismay. We are told that Lord North fell back as if struck by a cannon ball, and gasped: "O God, it is all over!"

Washington's Headquarters at Newburgh.

Although the War of Independence was really over, and several Americans went to Europe to settle the terms of peace, British troops staid in America some time longer, and kept possession of Savannah and Charleston about a year. Washington, therefore, did not dare dismiss his army. To keep better guard over the British at New York, he collected all his forces at Newburgh. But although there was no more fighting, Washington's presence was more sorely needed than ever, for the men, having received only a small part of their long-promised pay, and unable to go home and work for their destitute families, were restless and discontented. In fact, even the officers thought Congress managed things badly, and wished to make Washington king.

Had Washington thought of himself more than of others, or been unduly ambitious, he could now have gone, at the head of the army, to overthrow Congress and take the power into his own hands, like Cæsar and Napoleon. But Washington was a real patriot, and had no thought beyond the good of his country. He therefore sent for his officers, and made them a little speech.

In reading a letter from a congressman, promising that they should receive their dues, he had to take out his glasses, and as he put them on he quietly begged them to excuse him, saying: "My eyes have grown dim in the service of my country, but I have never doubted her justice." In his address he urged them not to tarnish the glory of their past services by rash conduct, and explained that Congress would soon settle their just demands. Such was the reliance placed upon his mere word, and the good influence he had over every man in his army, that all now consented to wait patiently until their services could receive their reward.

While Washington was thus keeping the soldiers in order, Franklin was in Europe, treating for peace. In 1782 George III. formally announced that he would recognize the independence of the United States, and closed his speech by saying he hoped that the same "religion, language, interests, and affections might prove a bond of permanent union between the two countries."

RESULTS OF THE WAR FOR INDEPENDENCE
BOUNDARY DEFINED BY TREATY 1783

The treaty, however, was signed in Paris, on the 3d of September, 1783. On this occasion Franklin donned the suit of Manchester velvet clothes which he had worn ten years before, when insulted in Parliament, and which he had vowed never to use again until his country was free. By this treaty the seacoast from Maine to Georgia was given up to the United States, together with all the land between the Great Lakes and Florida, westward as far as the Mississippi. At the same time, the British gave Florida back to Spain.

The news of this treaty was followed by the departure of the British soldiers from New York. They sailed away, leaving their flag still floating from the top of the liberty pole. Here some soldiers had nailed it fast, carefully greasing the pole so that the Americans should not haul down their colors until they were at least out of sight.

But a clever New York boy, seeing that it was useless to try to climb the greased pole in the usual way, ran into a neighboring store, and soon came back with a pocket full of nails, some cleats, and a hammer. Nailing a cleat a short distance up, he stood upon it to nail another still higher, and, climbing thus from point to point, reached the top of the pole, tore off the British flag, and replaced it by the American colors, amid the cheers of the assembled people!

LXXXIV. WASHINGTON'S FAREWELL.

Washington had already disbanded his army in Newburgh, when, on the eighth anniversary of the battle of Lexington, the war was formally declared to be over. Now, the British having gone, it remained only to bid farewell to his officers. On this occasion he said: "With a heart full of love and gratitude I now take leave of you. I most devoutly wish that your latter days may be as prosperous as your former have been glorious and honorable. I cannot come to each of you to take my leave, but I shall be obliged to you if each of you will come and take me by the hand."

General Knox was the first to advance, and Washington drew him toward him and kissed him. He also embraced all the rest—in dead silence, for all hearts were too full for speech. The officers then followed him to the boat and silently watched him out of sight. From New York, where this parting took place, Washington went direct to Annapolis, where, on the 23d of December, 1783, he received the formal message: "The United States, in Congress assembled, is prepared to receive the communications of the commander in chief." Washington then appeared before that body to lay down the heavy charge which he had borne so bravely for nearly eight years. He again refused to accept any reward for his services but handed over the exact account of his expenses, proving that he had spent more than sixty-three thousand dollars of his own money for the good of his country.

Then he went back to his farm at Mount Vernon, to take up again his usual work. He had been longing to do this for some time, for farming was his chief pleasure. Knowing this, his officers formed a society of which they made him head. They called themselves the Cincin-na′ti, in honor of a Roman patriot, Cincinnatus, who left his plow to save his country from danger, but hurried back to it as soon as the war was over.

The Mount Vernon House, South Front.

Instead of other pay, many of these officers and of the continental soldiers now received grants of land in what was then called the Northwest Territory. There they soon settled, working hard, and serving their country just as nobly by being good farmers, good citizens, good husbands, and good fathers as they had done by being good soldiers in the Revolutionary War. Before long, towns sprang up in the wilderness, and one of them was named Cincinnati, in honor of the society of which Washington was the first president.

But there were others besides the soldiers who were anxious to get back to their families. Foremost among these was the worthy Franklin, who had spent nearly nine years in France, looking after the interests of his country. He had seen the Peace of Paris signed; and when he reached Philadelphia, just sixty-two years after his first visit, he was welcomed with loud cheers and great rejoicings. He deserved all the cheering and honors he received, for he had been second only to Washington in the services he had rendered his beloved country.

As it was now decided beyond doubt that the former colonies were to be free states, independent of Great Britain, the Story of the Thirteen Colonies is ended. There is still to be told the Story of the Great Republic which was formed from these colonies, and which has grown to be one of the foremost nations in the world.

CPSIA information can be obtained
at www.ICGtesting.com
Printed in the USA
LVOW01s0601020516

486184LV00024B/744/P